Offering of Suffering

Offering of Suffering

Offer Your Suffering With His
For the Salvation of Souls
"Don't Waste Your Pain"

Paul A. Mihalik, OCDS, M. Ed.
Lt. Col. USAF (Ret)

Queenship
PUBLISHING COMPANY
P.O. Box 220 • Goleta, CA 93116
(800) 647-9882 • (805) 692-0043 • Fax: (805) 967-5843

Dedication

This book is dedicated to the Mother of God, Mary Most Holy, who, through her incomparable sufferings, participated with her Son in the Redemption of mankind.

> "If any man will come after Me, let him deny himself *and take up his cross*, and follow Me. For he that will save his life, will lose it, and he that shall lose his life *for my sake,* shall find it." Matt. 16:24-25

Library of Congress Number 00-135864

Published by:
Queenship Publishing
P.O. Box 220
Goleta, CA 93116
(800) 647-9882 • (805) 692-0043 • Fax: (805) 967-5843

Printed in the United States of America

ISBN: 1-57918-157-05

Contents

Chapter One

Suffering, Offered in the State of Grace, is Redemptive

The Morning Offering

"O Jesus, Through the Immaculate Heart Of Mary, I offer You all my prayers, works, and sufferings of this day, for the intentions of Your Sacred Heart, in union with all the Masses throughout the world, in reparation for all my sins, for the intentions of all our associates, and, in particular, for the intention of the Holy Father."

The prayer above, before Vatican Council II, was known by almost every Catholic, but is hardly known today. We are losing the very sense of sin today, let alone are we making reparation for our sins. We will see in the following chapters that the Virgin Mary has requested that the world make reparation for the sins against God.

In the Morning Offering, considered to be almost the perfect prayer of offering (Mass is the perfect offering), we apply the prayers, works, and sufferings in reparation *and for the conversion of souls.*

These are extremely worthy purposes. They bear supernatural fruit. Can we place a value on such power from a simple prayer? As we know, it is the intention that counts, not so much the action itself. Among the "works" spoken of are included our physical pain, mental anguish, joy, humiliations, disappointments, rejections — every emotion that comprises our daily life.

It is not simply a Catholic custom that puts credence and credibility into our sacrificial offerings. St. Paul says, "In my flesh I complete what is lacking in Christ's afflictions for the sake of His body, that is, the Church." Paul was referring to his physical and spiritual sufferings that were associated with and a result of his ministry.

The Church is very careful to point out to us that Christ's Passion and death on the Cross is alone sufficient and complete a sacrifice for the Redemption of mankind. Then what does Paul mean by his words? The answer is found in the understanding of the meaning of His Mystical Body on earth, which is the Church.

Christ's baptized followers make up the Mystical Body of Christ on earth, and Jesus is its Head. Christ's body suffered in the Passion and on the Cross. His "body" still suffers in a mysterious way in the pains and tribulations of followers. The pains and sufferings stem from the evil committed throughout the world. This evil is from the sins against God — the violation of His Commandments, especially those sins that interfere with the love of God and the love of neighbor. When we don't love, we sin!

Mankind is redeemed but mankind needs conversion. Man needs to be repentant. Man needs to make reparation, that is, to repair that which was broken and defiled. Man needs a change in behavior which starts in his heart until he can take up his cross and follow Him. This means the real follower of Jesus is destined to share in His sufferings if he is to be called a Christian, if he or she is to be saved, if he or she is to spend eternity in Heaven with the Father, Son, and Holy Spirit.

Reparation

Returning for a moment to the word — reparation; our offerings (or sacrifices, penances, atonements) make satisfaction to God for our sins. This need for reparation remains even though the guilt of our sin is forgiven in the sincere confession of a truly repentant sinner. Our conscience must be guided by the Ten Commandments and not what we think or "feel" is a sin. Restoration to the state of grace after grievous sin can be made by perfect contrition, **but Sacramental Confession is** *still* **required before receiving Holy Communion.**

No offering gains merit if one is not in the state of grace — that is, one must be *certain* to be restored to the friendship of God after having willfully ruptured this friendship with sin. A gift from one who has turned their back on you is hardly worth accepting unless you know the guilty party has seen their error and once again *wants* to restore the friendship. Sacramental Confession does this for the Catholic and is the only *certain* way one can be sure the relationship is restored. Why? Because it is very, very difficult to know for certain that one has perfect contrition, which requires a sincere and profound hatred for even venial sin.

So, the surest way is the way Jesus established for the Church. "Whose sins you shall forgive, are forgiven them. Whose sins you shall retain are retained." Clearly, someone is to forgive in His name, and He spoke to the Apostles, His first priests, when He established this Sacrament of Reconciliation. And clearly, a judgment cannot be made by the priest to forgive or retain unless the priest *hears* the nature of the sin from the sinner personally.

So we confess, and are forgiven, and return to the arms of the Father, and can once again offer our prayers, and sacrifices, and works in reparation and for the conversion of sinners. We once again receive merit for our intentions to bring healing to the Mystical Body of Christ as He is on earth, in the Church — "In my flesh I complete what is lacking ... for the sake of His Body, that is, the Church." In this way we can bring healing (reparation) to His Body that suffered for us.

Even after a "good" confession, some degree of reparation is usually required in addition to any penance assigned by the priest. It is this reparation that we want to make up. In the case of stealing, compensation must be made if possible. In other sins, reparation is offered in the form of sacrifices, or acts of generosity, or fasting, etc. It is this kind of reparation Jesus accepts as atonement for our sins. It always includes prayer, adoration, praise, and charity.

Not only do we offer our works, prayers, and sufferings *to Him* — we actually *join our sufferings with His* to be offered to the Father because Jesus accepts them. (See Chapter Three, The Apostolic Letter of Pope John Paul II on Redemptive Suffering, for a detailed explanation of the theological basis for our privilege to mysteriously make reparation and participate in the salvation of souls through our personal redemptive suffering.) The title might sound formidable but the reader is strongly encouraged to read carefully what the Holy Father has to say.

As the Vicar of Christ on earth and successor of Peter, his words require our closest attention and compliance. We are obligated to comply with his letters to the faithful even if they have not been formally issued "Ex-cathedra" (from the chair of Peter), as dogma. Fr. Groeschel, the frequent host on Mother Angelica's television network, has said that we really cannot call ourselves Catholic if we do not heed the Holy Father's encyclicals. The apostolic letters fall into a similar category as concerns the Pope's guidance to his flock. We ignore his teachings at our own spiritual peril.

A Beautiful and Healthy Belief

Growing from our knowledge that God is a truly loving and forgiving Father, we believe that He listens to and accepts our apologies (repentance for sin). And deep in our human makeup is the need to restore the peace and joy that has been disrupted in a once loving relationship. Sin does a lot of disrupting. The breaking of the Commandments and the deliberate and knowing turning away from Jesus's teachings is a sure way of losing our internal peace and it gives rise to feelings of guilt if our conscience is alert to what sin really is and how much it really does offend God.

The desire to make amends for our transgressions should eventually draw us to deep sorrow for our sins and to Sacramental Confession. We, as sinners, need desperately to remember that Jesus said we are to forgive not just seven times but seventy times seven and more if needed. He is a teacher that practices what He preaches and we should never ever avoid Confession because we think we have worn out our welcome or that in some twisted way of thinking, we are beyond His forgiveness — which then becomes a case of despair and can lead to the certain loss of the soul. The Sacred Heart, in appearances to St. Gertrude the Great and other Saints made it clear that although Christ is in His glory in Heaven, He and His Mother suffer great pain and anguish over sin and the loss of souls. This is a mystery that is beyond our comprehension but we might begin to understand the possibility of His anguish when we think about His Passion and death on the Cross and yet millions of souls reject His gift of eternal life. A victim soul, one chosen by Jesus to voluntarily suffer for the conversion of sinners, was a nun named Sr. Josefa Menendez who died in 1923. This nun's story is contained in a book which is based on her diary. In this book she describes the great suffering that Jesus still personally undergoes. He would appear to her with all His wounds bleeding profusely, wearing His crown of thorns, with the open wound in His side, and nail holes in His hands gaping and bleeding, and He would ask Josefa if she would help ease His sufferings by taking on part of His own for the sake of saving souls. This is basically what redemptive suffering from us human beings is all about. Some insights into the whys and wherefores of this victim soul business and the offering of our human pains and sufferings might be gained when the reader studies Chapter Six, which discusses Sr. Josefa and her horrible but yet beautiful journey for saving souls. Each of us can contribute to some degree to the saving of souls when we understand the concept of redemptive suffering.

Chapter Six and Chapter Seven will discuss the great suffering of St. Therese of Lisieux and Blessed Padre Pio, another victim Soul who bore the wounds of Christ for fifty years in the quest for saving souls.

Mental Health

From the standpoint of psychology and sound mental health the Sacrament of Reconciliation is a priceless gift from God. It is a great and special privilege to be able to say to a loving and infinitely patient Heavenly Father, "I am sorry and I truly desire to make amends and to prove my sorrow and my love for You." The benefit to mental health is from the certainty that we are heard and forgiven and this forgiveness is available time and time again so long as our repentance is genuine. Jesus told Sr. Josefa, "Once a sin is confessed I no longer remember the sin unless it is repeated." Even so, we are obligated to make reparation for the broken covenant. Sacramental Confession gives us the "guarantee" that we are once again received in the open arms of Jesus and the Father. Jesus accepts our sorrow and once again we are His heirs of Heaven. We are expected to make a firm purpose of amendment; our contrition must never be a frivolous thing. Knowing that, as sinners, we can fall again and again and be forgiven again and again contributes to our ability to live a more integrated life with a minimum of paralyzing guilt so we can be free to make progress in our daily attempt to grow in holiness. God knew his creature, man, would need such a healing Sacrament and He gave it to us. Isn't it an amazing puzzlement that most of them avoid it?

It is a recognized fact that many mental health therapists acknowledge that the overall mental health of the Catholic population was much better when Sacramental Confession to a priest was almost a weekly habit for us in the pre-Vatican II period. Approximately only three percent of Catholics now participate in the Sacrament at least monthly. When was the last time you were encouraged from the pulpit to attend the Sacrament of Reconciliation, other perhaps than Easter or Christmas? Physical and mental healings, in addition to spiritual healings, have been know to take place immediately after confessing to a priest. There is a connection between healing and the Sacrament of Reconciliation. Certainly the soul is made well and if it be the will of God, other forms of healing can take place. Only fools avoid what is good for them. Why do so-called intelligent believers deliberately avoid a source of grace, healing, and salvation? The answer to that question might explain the problems in the Church since Vatican Council II. The lack of priestly vocations for over 30 years, the disappearance of the nuns and the ever growing lack of a sense of sin, even among Catholics, as evidenced by the small numbers attending Confession, and renegade bishops hint of serious problems that will take years to overcome, if ever.

Some bishops and theologians do not want one, Holy, Catholic, and Apostolic Church!

Chapter Two

"Deny Thyself, Take Up Thy Cross and Follow Me"

Matt. 16:24-25

The contents of this book are intended to help bring to those who suffer in any form whatsoever, a realization that their suffering **need not be in vain,** even in the face of certain death from terminal illnesses. Hopefully, the reader will discover that although there is no magic potion to lessen the pain of physical, psychological, or spiritual suffering we do not have to feel the remainder of our lives is so much wasted effort where we don't count anymore and we can't contribute to the well-being of ourselves and, more importantly, to others. Suffering can be a sublime gift. Look at the fruit of the sacrifice of Jesus on the Cross. It surprises many to learn that our sufferings too can be "offered," and offered for the same reason Jesus died on the Cross, to assist in the plan of saving souls.

When Jesus spoke to the crowds and said they would have everlasting life if they would eat His body and drink His blood, and they interpreted this to mean some form of cannibalism, some sickened and rebelled against Him, and finally deserted Him and His Gospel. Many Christians feel just as strongly about the idea of redemptive suffering, that suffering offered by Christians for the sake of their own sins and for the conversion of souls. They reject totally this concept, that no one's suffering but that of the Redeemer can be applied to the saving of souls. Almost everyone recognizes the value of prayer to that purpose, but not to the purpose of saving souls. It is hoped that those who think this way will read on to find the theological justification for believing that you and I can help save souls through the offering of our sufferings to God.

There are all kinds of suffering: rejection by friends or loved ones, humiliations, disappointments, injustices, prejudices, discrimination, unfounded criticisms, not being appreciated, being taken for granted by those who mean the most to us, and of course, grief and physical pain; the last two, perhaps, being the most difficult to live with. For many, they can not see in their sufferings the will of God in their lives for them. They refuse to see that, for all of us, suffering, can be a calling to a beautiful ministry, a means to cooperate with God in the saving of souls. This vocation is not limited only to bishops, priests, religious, and martyrs. This is a vocation for all the members of the Mystical Body of Christ. One can understand this if they are aware of the depth of the love and mercy which God has for every single human being. He grants us the privilege of helping in His glorious plan of redemption. Understanding this concept might be the only way we can understand the answer to the question — Why does God permit or cause the innocent to suffer when those seen as evil by their actions seem to reap all kinds of blessings in this life — blessings of good health, amazing wealth, and fantastically successful careers. St. Paul explained the value of his personal sufferings for "Christ's Body, the Church" (Col 1:24) Pope John Paul II expands on this in his *Apostolic Letter on Suffering* in Chapter Three, an extremely important chapter to help understand why suffering should be seen as a sublime gift and privilege.

Understanding this concept can help us accept sufferings without getting angry with God; it can save us from the deadly hopelessness of despair. It gives purpose to those in hospital beds, wheelchairs, and in prisons. It might be surprising for some to know that, in addition to prayer, every human and spiritual experience can be offered to God in expiation for our personal sins and for the salvation of souls.

This morning at Mass, the celebrant, Fr. Michael Stallings, was speaking of the power we have in us — a power that comes from

God. He said "we can be creators, making good things happen; that like artists, we can make life beautiful for those around us — sometimes with our hands and always with our love of others." Another dimension of this *creating good* is the offering of our sufferings for others. Can there be a more Christlike action on our part than to share in Christ's suffering for the sake of others? This is the essence of being a Christian — to be a follower of Christ — to be Christlike. "Since Christ suffered physically, you too must strengthen yourselves with the same way of thinking that He had; because whoever suffers physically is no longer involved with sin. From now on you must spend the rest of your earthly lives controlled by God's will and not by human desires." (1 Peter:4:1, 2) In other words, suffering might become our lot as willed by God and we should have no desires contrary to His will in the matter. Knowing God's will in the matter is not always easy. We are expected to do all in our power and through modern medicine to look for healing if our cross is one of physical or mental suffering. If these resources fail, we can deduce from this that it is God's will for us to carry that cross which is very specifically designed for us personally.

In suffering, we actually share in Christ's sufferings and for the very same purpose He suffered. "My dear friends, do not be surprised at the painful test you are suffering as though something unusual were happening to you. Rather, be glad that you are sharing Christ's sufferings, that you may be full of joy when His glory is revealed." (1 Peter 4:12, 13). His glory will be revealed in His Kingdom to all who are saved, *and they were saved by His sufferings!*

"For you have been given the privilege of serving Christ, not only by believing in Him, but also in suffering for Him." (Phil 1:29) "All of you are Christ's body and each one of you is part of it." (1 Cor 13:27). Each one of us can expect suffering in some form if we are, as individuals, part of His body. This is synonymous with being "Christ-like."

Let's look at the Morning Offering prayer again to see the specifics of that offering: O Jesus, through the Immaculate Heart of Mary, I offer You all my prayers, works, and sufferings of this day; for all the intentions of Your Sacred Heart — (His intentions are always that every soul would seek salvation of their own free will; He died for that).

"...in union with the Holy Sacrifice of the Mass throughout the world, in reparation for my sins, for the intention of our associates, and, in particular, for the intention of the Holy Father. Amen."

This prayer has the Imprimatur of Leo C. Byrne, Coadjutor Archbishop of St. Paul and Minneapolis. This tells us that the prayer is free of any theological error. It means the Church officially recommends that, not only our prayers be offered to God, but all our works and sufferings for our sins and those of our associates.... There is a recognized value of these offerings especially *when offered in union with all the Masses throughout the world this day.*

This joining of our prayers, works, and sufferings with the Masses sanctifies and elevates our offerings to an infinite value because *they are joined with Christ's death in the bloodless sacrifice of the Mass.* Christ accepts our offerings and offers it with Himself to the Father who accepts it for the reparation of sin and the salvation of souls.

In this way our daily lives with all our experiences, and no matter how unimportant they are in themselves, become a source of inestimable treasure when offered with Christ's sufferings. God the Father is only too willing to receive them in His plan of salvation. He receives them as a sign of our love for Him, our gratitude, our thoughtfulness, our compassion for His Son's suffering, and our acknowledgement of all His gifts to us. Our lives take on a whole and beautiful meaning in the light of its being offered as a sacrifice to the Creator. We rise above the level of just being simply a created being. We become, as heirs of Heaven in Baptism, participants in God's plan of Redemption. For those who cannot preach the Gospel or shed their blood as martyrs, or serve as priests or religious, they can never again say their lives are of no real use on this earth. It is within the reach of every soul to become participants in the plan of Redemption. What a sublime purpose to live for and to suffer for!.

Later, in Chapters Six, Seven, and Eight we will discuss the heroic lives of three victim souls who were called by God to offer tremendous pain and suffering for the salvation of souls. Two were victims of His justice and one was a victim of His love. For now we will introduce the heroic lives of the two recently beatified children of Fatima, Blessed Francisco and Blessed Jacinta, ages eight and seven respectively when the Virgin Mary appeared to them on May 13, 1917.

Blessed Francisco and Blessed Jacinta

The two Blesseds of Fatima, Francisco and Jacinta, came to fully understand the concept of making sacrifices for the conversion of souls and in reparation for sin, in spite of their young ages. They were two good but rather ordinary children before God's Angel appeared to them and their cousin Lucy (still alive at age 90), in 1916.

The Angel of Portugal

A little know fact about the Fatima apparitions is the visitation of the Angel of Portugal to the children three times before the Blessed Mother appeared to them. Sr. Lucia did not divulge this information until long after the apparitions ceased. The Angel's role was to teach the children about the critical need for us to offer reparation for sin and to pray for sinners. On his second visit the Angel told the children, "...Pray. Pray a great deal! The Hearts of Jesus and Mary have designs of mercy on you. Offer up prayers and sacrifices to the Most High." They replied, "How are we to make sacrifices?" He answered, *"Make everything you do* a sacrifice, and offer it as an act of reparation for the sins by which he is offended, and in supplication for the conversion of sinners. Bring peace to your country in this way. I am its Angel Guardian, the Angel of Portugal. Above all, *accept and bear with submission the sufferings sent you by Our Lord."* There it is for us to grab on to and chew a while. "Make *everything* you do a sacrifice!" Prayer, works, sufferings can all be offered in sacrifice!.

The Angel is a messenger and the message came from God. "Offer up prayers and sacrifices to the Most High." The sacrifices were to specifically be offered in reparation for sin and the conversion of souls. The children can also be considered to be victim souls. They were selected by God to "accept and bear with submission the sufferings sent you by Our Lord." Can our minds grasp the momentous meaning of this request? Children of ages seven and eight (Lucia was ten), being asked to accept with submission the sufferings God would send to them? Can we understand 1) why would God send suffering to the children, and 2) why to innocent children? These questions will be answered in the following chapters that include the apostolic letter of Pope John Paul II where he amplifies the words of St. Paul, "And now I am happy about my sufferings for you, for by means of my physical sufferings, I am helping to complete what still remains of Christ's sufferings, on behalf of His body, the Church." (Col. 1:24) And each individual one of us is a member of that "body." We suffer for one another as we suffer for Christ. "And so there is no division, but all its different parts have the same concern for one another. If one part of the body suffers, all the other parts suffer with it: if one part is praised, all the other parts share its happiness." (1 Cor. 12:25, 26)

Lucia said about the words of the Angel on making sacrifices, "These words made a deep impression on our minds, like a light making us understand who God is, how He loves us and desires to be loved, as well as the value of sacrifice, how pleasing it is to him, and, how, on account of it, He grants the grace of conversion to sinners. For this reason, from that moment, we began to offer up all that mortified us, never seeking other ways of mortification and penance, except to remain for hours with our foreheads touching the ground, repeating the prayer the Angel taught us."

Request of Mary For Sacrifices At Third Apparition on July 13, 1917

On July 13, 1917, Our Lady told the seers, "Sacrifice ourselves for sinners and say often, especially when you make some sacrifice, 'O Jesus, this is for love of You, for the conversion of sinners, and in reparation for the sins committed against the Immaculate Heart of Mary.'"

At the fourth apparition of Our Lady on August 13, 1917, Our Lady told the children, "Pray, pray very much and make sacrifices for sinners, for many souls go to hell because they have nobody to pray and make sacrifices for them."

When Jesus said we are to deny ourselves, take up our cross and follow Him, He used the word *cross* to represent all that life on earth consists of for the descendants of Adam and Eve. We are destined to live with difficulties of all sorts because of what we lost as a result of the sin of our first parents. The "cross" is another word for what we can expect as part of everyday life. What are some of these crosses that Jesus will accept as sacrifices, mortifications, sufferings, offerings, and penances?

Two selections are presented from outstanding writings that describe in detail the daily crosses that belabor mankind, the kind most will experience on earth and which we can offer to God for ourselves and others. The first selection is made up of excerpts from the beautiful book *My Daily Bread* by Fr. Anthony J. Paone, S.J., published by the Confraternity of the Precious Blood in 1954 with the imprimatur of Thomas Edmundus Malloy, S.T.D., Archbishop of Brooklyn:

Christ speaks:

> "My child ... you cannot eliminate the unexpected, the unforeseen, and the unavoidable. In many cases your best remedy and weapon will be an intelligent patience with yourself as well as with others.
>
> "Every man has his daily share of troubles and trials. Sometimes it may be bodily pain and discomfort. At other times it may be mental or spiritual suffering, some annoyance, disappointment, or anxiety. Sometimes you may feel that I have deserted you. Then again you may have to bear misunderstandings, misinterpretations, and even bad will from your neighbor.
>
> "Every one would like to be free of these trials but it cannot be. They are part of your earthly life. Wherever you turn, you will always find my cross in one form or another.
>
> "My child ... believe Me. It is a great mistake to expect anything else but suffering and hardship in this life! Man's earthly life is full of miseries and crosses. Wherever you turn, you will find a cross.

"If you carry it willingly, you will find greater strength in the cross, and it will lead you towards heaven. If you bear it unwillingly you only make it a greater burden than it already is; and you still have to carry it. One who runs away from the cross is only running towards another cross, perhaps even a heavier one.

"There is no other road to heaven except the way of the cross. No man can escape his cross. Even My saints went through their earthly life burdened by the cross. Not a single hour of My earthly life was free of the cross. I entered into My glory by My suffering and dying upon the cross. Do not fear the cross. I shall help you bear it.

"Be a good and loyal soldier of mine. Be determined to embrace your cross for love of Me. I warn you now that if you are resolved to prove your love for me, you can only do it by embracing your daily cross of annoyances, labors, disappointments, opposition, and even different forms of persecution. The higher you rise in true and solid virtue, the more easily you will recognize crosses and embrace them. In fact, as your love for me grows, so too will your love for the cross.... If there were anything better than the cross, would I not have chosen it? That is why I commanded: 'If anyone wishes to come after Me, Let him deny himself, take up his cross daily, and follow Me.'

"Never forget for a moment this truth: through many trials will you enter into the kingdom of Heaven. Therefore, take up your cross daily and follow Me. I will not permit anything in your life which does not help your higher interests.... It is My love for you which makes Me treat you as I do. Your present trials and sufferings are as much My gift as the satisfaction and consolation which I send you."

The second selection of writings is from *The Divine Intimacy* by Fr. Gabriel of St. Mary Magdalen, O.C.D. This Carmelite priest was a great spiritual director for many and this book of his is considered to be a classic in spirituality. Published by Tan Books and Publishers in Boston in 1964. The imprimatur is by Richard Cardinal Cushing, Archbishop of Boston:

The following is a clear explanation of how our personal sufferings, applied through the mystery of the Mystical Body of Christ, can bear good fruit, that is, reparation for sins and the conversion of souls:

"I ... fill up those things that are wanting of the suffering of Christ, in my flesh, for His Body, which is the Church." (Col. 1-24) This is another motive which has urged the saints to generous corporal mortification. Nothing is lacking in the Passion of Christ; He himself said, 'All is consummated.' All was accomplished in Him, our Head, but it must now be accomplished in us, His members.

Jesus wills to continue His Passion in us so that we may be associated with Him in the work of redemption; He wills to make us His collaborators in the most sublime of His works, the salvation of souls. Jesus, Who could have accomplished his work alone, willed to need us in order to apply the infinite merits of his Passion to many souls.

Mortifications, and even physical suffering, is therefore a requirement of a life of union with Christ; the more generous the soul is, the more will it participate intimately in the interior life and the apostolic work of Jesus. We cannot be intimate with Christ, if we do not suffer with Him, if we do not ascend the cross with Him....

Suffering has a supernatural value only when it is borne with Christ and for Christ. It is Jesus who sanctifies suffering; apart from him it is worth nothing and is of no use. But if it is embraced for love of Him, it becomes precious coin, capable of redeeming and sanctifying souls; it becomes a continuation of the Passion.

...The word *Cross* should not make us think of only special sufferings which, while not excluded, are not generally our portion. First of all we must think of those common daily disagreeable things which are part of everyday life.... These may include physical ailments caused by poor health, economic restrictions, fatigue attendant upon overwork or anxiety; they may be moral sufferings resulting from differences of opinion, clash of temperaments or misunderstandings. Herein lies the genuine cross that Jesus offers us daily.

The value, the fruitfulness of our daily sacrifices comes from this unreserved acceptance, which makes us receive them just as God offers them to us, without trying to avoid them or to lessen their weight.... All are part of the divine plan. All, even the tiniest, have been predisposed by God from all eternity for our salvation. Every suffering, whatever its dimensions, always conceals a redemptive, a sanctifying grace; and this grace becomes ours from the moment we accept the suffering in a spirit of faith, for the love of God.

We have presented considerable evidence that Jesus desires that His followers emulate Him in suffering and that our suffering is not in vain when we accept it as the will of God in our lives and utilize it for souls. In the next chapter we will read the words of Pope John Paul II as He gives an expanded justification on the positive aspects of human suffering. We will see the teaching of the Church on this subject which is taken to heart by those desirous of saving souls and making reparation. The reader might prefer to return later to study the Holy Father's guidance on the subject of offering our sufferings, and continue on to chapter four which deals with the heroic acts of Blessed Francisco and Blessed Jacinta in favor of sinners.

We will close this chapter by again reading the words of the Blessed Virgin Mary in Fatima in 1917, to emphasize the urgent need for us to make reparation and pray for the salvation of sinners. This book is intended to be an appeal to those who suffer to offer those sufferings as their reply to Jesus and Mary:

*Sacrifice y*ourselves for sinners, and say often, especially when you make some sacrifice, "O Jesus, this is for the love of You, for the conversion of sinners, and in reparation for the sins committed against the Immaculate Heart of Mary." Pray, pray very much and make sacrifices for many souls go to hell because they have nobody to pray and make sacrifices for them.

Offering of Suffering

Chapter Three

From the Apostolic Letter
Salvifici Doloris (The Christian
Meaning of Suffering)

— Pope John Paul II, February 11, 1984

In the following excerpts from his Apostolic Letter the Holy Father amplifies on St. Paul's words on the meaning of suffering. The Pope makes these points to enlighten us and encourage us to participate in the ministry of suffering for souls and making reparation as seen in the mind of the Church:

1. Christ accepted His sufferings as the will of the Father for Him.

2. Christ's sufferings are the proof of His love for mankind.

3. Christ asked at Gethsemene that His sufferings might pass from Him, which proved that suffering was then seen as an evil.

4. Christ's words attest to the incomparable suffering that the Man who is truly the only begotten Son of God could experience.

5. Christ's words help us to understand the difference as well as the similarity that exists between every possible form of human suffering and the suffering of the God-man.

6. Christ's words on Golgotha express the sincerity of His suffering when he asks His Father "My God, My God. Why have

You forsaken Me?" because of our sins laid on Him — the iniquity of us all.

7. Precisely because of this suffering Christ brings about the Redemption and He can say, "It is finished."

8. Christ's death gives new meaning to all forms of suffering. It is no longer an evil but is now intercessory and redemptive.

9. St. Paul teaches that we become sharers in Christ's suffering "for the sake of Christ" and that we share in the work of redemption. He says we are to present our bodies "as a living sacrifice, holy and acceptable to God." (Rom. 12:1)

10. St. Paul teaches that to share in the suffering of Christ is at the same time to suffer for the Kingdom of God and we become worthy of that Kingdom.

11. St. Paul writes that "We are ... fellow heirs of Christ provided that we suffer with Him in order that we may be glorified in Him." (Rom. 8:17, 18)

12. Although the Redemption achieved by Christ is complete, this Redemption accomplished through His love, remains open to all love that is expressed in human suffering, and in this manner, the Redemption, mysteriously, is always being accomplished.

13. Suffering is truly supernatural as well as human. It is supernatural because it has its roots in the Redemption of the world. It is human because a person discovers himself, his own humanity, his own dignity, and his own salvific mission.

Excerpts From *Salvifici Doloris* by Pope John Paul II:

...One can say that with the passion of Christ all human suffering has found itself in a new situation....

The Redeemer suffered in place of man and for man. Every man has his own share in the Redemption. Each one is also called to share in that suffering through which the Redemption was accomplished. He is called to share in that suffering through which all human suffering has also been redeemed. In bringing about the Redemption through suffering, Christ has also raised human suffering to the level of the Redemption. Thus each man in his suffering, can also become a sharer in the redemptive suffering of Christ.

...If one becomes a sharer in the sufferings of Christ, it happens because Christ has opened his suffering to man, because he Himself in His redemptive suffering, has become, in a certain sense, a sharer in all human suffering. Man discovering through faith the redemptive suffering of Christ, also discovers in it his own sufferings; he rediscovers them, through faith, enriched with a new content and new meaning.... The cross of Christ throws salvific light, in a most penetrating way, on man's life and in particular on his suffering.

In the eyes of the just God, before His judgment, those who share in the suffering of Christ become worthy of His kingdom. Through their sufferings, in a certain sense, they repay the infinite price of the passion and death of Christ, which became the price of our Redemption: at this price the kingdom of God has become consolidated anew in human history, becoming the definitive prospect of man's earthly existence.... Christ has led us into the kingdom through His suffering. And also through suffering those surrounded by the mystery of Christ's Redemption became mature enough to enter this kingdom.

...Suffering is also an invitation to manifest the moral greatness of man, his spiritual maturity. Proof of this has been given ... by the martyrs and confessors of Christ who were faithful to his words: "And do not fear those who kill the body, but cannot kill the soul."

"Now I rejoice in my sufferings for your sake, and in my flesh I complete what is lacking in Christ's afflictions for the sake of his body, that is, the Church." (Col. 1:24)

In another letter to the Colossians, Paul writes, 'Do you not know that your bodies are members of Christ?' (1 Cor. 6:15)

The mystery of the church is expressed in this: that already in the act of baptism, which brings about a configuration with Christ, and then through His sacrifice, sacramentally through the Eucharist — the Church is continually being built up spiritually as the Body of Christ. In this Body, Christ wishes to be united with every individual, and, in a special way, he is united with those who suffer. There is an exceptional nature of this union. Whoever suffers in union with Christ just as the Apostle Paul bears his "tribulations" in union with Christ not only receives from Christ that strength already referred to but also completes by his suffering "what is lacking in Christ's afflictions."

The sufferings of Christ created the good of the world's Redemption. This good in itself is inexhaustible and infinite. No man can add anything to it. But, at the same time, in the mystery of the Church as His body, Christ has, in a sense, opened His own redemptive suffering to all human suffering. Insofar as man becomes a sharer in Christ's sufferings in any part of the world and at any time in history, to that extent he in his own way completes the suffering through which Christ accomplished the Redemption of the world.

Does this mean that the Redemption of Christ is not complete? No. It only means that the Redemption, accomplished through satisfactory love, remains always open to all love expressed in human suffering. In this dimension, the dimension of love, the Redemption which has already been completely accomplished is, in a certain sense, constantly being accomplished. Christ achieved the Redemption completely and to the very limit; but at the same time He did not bring it to a close. In this redemptive suffering, through which the Redemption of the world has been accomplished, Christ opened Himself from the beginning to every human suffering and constantly does so. Yes, it seems to be part of the very essence of Christ's redemptive suffering that this suffering requires to be unceasingly completed.

Thus, with this openness to every human suffering, Christ has accomplished the world's Redemption through His own suffering. For, at the same time, this redemption, even though it was completely achieved by Christ's suffering, lives on and in its own special way develops in the history of man. It lives and develops as the Body of Christ, the Church, and in this dimension every human suffering, by reason of the loving union with Christ, completes the suffering of Christ. It completes that suffering just as the Church completes the redemptive work of Christ. The mystery of the Church, that body which completes in itself also Christ's crucified and risen body indicates, at the same time, the space or context in which human sufferings complete the sufferings of Christ. Only within this radius and dimension of the Church as the Body of Christ, which continually develops in space and time, can one think and speak of "what is lacking" in the sufferings of Christ. The Apostle Paul, in fact, make this clear when he writes of "completing what is lacking in Christ's afflictions for the sake of His body, that is, the Church."

...This also highlights the divine and human nature of the Church. Suffering seems in some way to share in the characteristics of this nature. And for this reason suffering also has a special value in the eyes of the church. It is something good, before which the Church bows down in reverence with all its depth of her faith in the Redemption. She likewise bows down with all the depth of that faith with which she embraces within herself the inexpressible mystery of the Body of Christ.

...This suffering, together with the living word of His teaching, become a rich source for all those who shared in Jesus' sufferings among the first generation of his disciples and confessors and among those who have come after them.

...Down the centuries and generations it has been seen that in suffering there is concealed a particular power that draws a person interiorly closer to Christ, a special grace. To this grace many saints, such as St. Francis of Assisi, St. Ignatius of Loyola and others, owe their profound conversion. A result of such a conversion is not only that the individual discovers the salvific meaning of suffering, but above all that he becomes a completely new person. He discovers a new dimension, as it were, of his entire life and vocation. This discovery is a particular confirmation of the spiritual greatness which in man surpasses the body in a way that is completely beyond compare. When this body is gravely ill, totally incapacitated, and the person is almost incapable of living and acting, all the more do interior maturity and spiritual greatness become evident, constituting a touching lesson to those who are healthy and normal.

This interior maturity and spiritual greatness in suffering are certainly the result of a particular conversion and cooperation with the grace of the crucified Redeemer. It is He Himself who acts at the heart of human sufferings through His spirit of truth, through the consoling Spirit. It is He who transforms, in a certain sense, the very substance of the spiritual life, indicating for the person who suffers a place close to Himself. It is He, as the interior Master and Guide, who reveals to the suffering brother and sister this wonderful interchange, situated at the very heart of the mystery of the Redemption. Suffering, is, in itself, an experience of evil. But Christ has made suffering the firmest basis of the definitive good, namely the good of eternal salvation ... suffering cannot be transformed and recharged by the grace from outside, but from within. And Christ, through His own salvific suffering is very much present in every human suffering, and acts from within on that suffering by the powers of the Holy Spirit of truth, His consoling Spirit.

...However, this interior process does not always follow the same pattern. It often begins and is set in motion with great difficulty. Even the very point of departure differs: people react to suffering in different ways. But in general it can be said that almost always the individual enters suffering with a typically human protest and with the question "why?" He asks the meaning of his suffering and seeks an answer to this question on the human level. Certainly he often puts this question to God, and to Christ. Furthermore, he cannot help noticing that the One to whom he puts the question is Himself suffering and wishes to answer him from the cross, from the heart of His own suffering. Nevertheless, it takes time, even a long time, for this answer to begin to be interiorly perceived. For Christ does not answer directly and he does not answer in the abstract this human questioning about the meaning of suffering. Man hears Christ's saving answer as he himself gradually become a sharer in the sufferings of Christ.

The answer which comes through this sharing, by way of the interior encounter with the Master, is in itself something more than the mere abstract answer to the question about the meaning of suffering. For it is above all a call. It is a vocation. Christ does not explain in the abstract the reasons for the suffering, but before all else He says "Follow Me. Come! Take part through your suffering in this work of saving the world, a salvation achieved through My suffering! Through My Cross!"

Gradually, as the individual takes up his cross, spiritually uniting himself to the cross of Christ, the salvific meaning of suffering is revealed before him.... He does not discover this meaning at his own human level, but at the level of the suffering of Christ. At the same time, however, from this level of Christ the salvific meaning of suffering descends to man's level and becomes, in a sense, the individual's personal response. It is then that man finds in his suffering interior peace and even spiritual joy.

(I interrupt the reader to point out that the essence of the Holy Father's message is summed up in the following paragraphs. These words are merciful and uplifting because they show us that suffering is truly a gift and provides for each one of us the opportunity to make reparation and participate in God's plan of salvation. This knowledge removes all reasons to be depressed and angry about our sufferings. To share this beautiful knowledge with those who suffer is the primary purpose of this book.)

St. Paul speaks of true joy in his letter to the Colossians: "I rejoice in my sufferings for your sake" (Col 1:24). A sense of joy is found in the overcoming of the sense of uselessness of suffering — a feeling that is sometimes very strongly rooted in human suffering. This feeling not only consumes the person interiorly, but seems to make him a burden to others. The person feels condemned to receive help and assistance from others and, at the same time, seems useless to himself.

The discovery of the salvific meaning of suffering in union with Christ transforms this depressing feeling. Faith in sharing in the suffering of Christ brings with it the certainty that the suffering person "completes what is lacking in Christ's afflictions;" the certainty that in the spiritual dimension of the work of redemption he is serving, like Christ, in the spiritual salvation of his brothers and sisters. Therefore, he is carrying out an irreplaceable service.

In the Body of Christ, which is ceaselessly born of the Cross of the Redeemer, it is precisely suffering permeated by the spirit of Christ's sacrifice that is the irreplaceable mediator and author of the good things which are indispensable for the world's salvation. It is suffering, more than anything else, which clears the way for the grace which transforms human souls.... Suffering, more than anything else makes present in the history of humanity, the powers of the Redemption. In that "cosmic" struggle between the spiritual powers of good and evil, spoken of in the letter to the Ephesians (Eph. 6:12), human sufferings, united to the redemptive sufferings of Christ, constitute a special support for the powers of good and open the way to victory of these salvific powers.

And so the Church sees in all Christ's suffering brothers and sisters as it were, a multiple subject of His supernatural power. How often is it precisely to them that the pastors of the Church appeal, and precisely from them that they seek help and support! The gospel of suffering is being written unceasingly with the words of this strange paradox: the springs of divine power gush forth precisely in the midst of human weakness. Those who share in the sufferings of Christ preserve in their own suffering a very special particle of the infinite treasure of the world's Redemption, *and can share this treasure with others.*

The more a person is threatened by sin, the heavier the structures of sin which today's world brings; the greater is the eloquence which human suffering possesses in itself and the more the Church feels the need to have recourse to the value of human sufferings for the salvation of the world.

Offering of Suffering

Chapter Four

The Voluntary Suffering of The Children of Fatima for Reparation and Conversion of Souls

Chosen first to be presented as outstanding examples of those who voluntarily suffer for souls are the children of Fatima, Jacinta, Francisco, and Lucia. If children aged 7, 8, and 10 can understand the concept of redemptive suffering, adults should be able to. Francisco and Jacinta, recently beatified by the Church, have been recognized officially for their heroic virtues manifested primarily in their sacrificial offerings of prayer, fasting, penances, and persecution.

These children were taught by the Angel of Portugal and the Blessed Virgin Mary that such sacrifices and prayers were urgently needed to restore peace in the world and for the salvation of souls. It is not uncommon for Marian apparitions to come to young people. "Father ... to you I offer praise, for what you have hidden from the learned and clever you have revealed to the merest of children." (Matt. 11:25)

On May 13, 2000, with six hundred thousand faithful gathered near the Basilica of Our Lady of the Rosary in Fatima, Pope John Paul beatified the servants of God, Francisco and Jacinta Martos.

The following words are taken from the Holy Father's homily of the Mass. They describe for us why these two were beatified:

One night, his Father (Francisco's), heard him sobbing and asked him why he was crying; his son answered, "I was thinking of Jesus who is so sad because of sins that are committed against Him." He was motivated by one desire — so expressive of how young children think — to console Jesus and make Him happy.... A transformation takes place in his life, one we would call radical; a transformation certainly uncommon for children of his age. He devotes himself to an intense spiritual life expressed in assiduous and fervent prayer, and attains a true form of mystical union with the Lord. This spurs him to a progressive purification of the spirit through the renunciation of his own pleasures and even of innocent childhood games.

Francisco bore without complaining the great suffering caused by the illness from which he died. It all seemed to him so little to console Jesus; he died with a smile on his lips. Little Francisco had a great desire to atone for the offenses of sinners by striving to be good and offering his sacrifices and prayers. The life of his younger sister by almost two years, was motivated by the same sentiments.

Little Jacinta felt and personally experienced Our Lady's anguish, offering herself heroically as a victim for sinners. One day, when she and Francisco had already contracted the flu that forced them to bed, the Virgin Mary came to visit them at home as the little Jacinta recounts: "Our Lady came to see us and said that soon she would come and take Francisco to Heaven. And she asked me if I still wanted to convert more sinners. I told her yes." And when the time came for Francisco to go to Heaven, the little girl tells him, "Give my greetings to Our Lord and to Our Lady and tell them that I am enduring everything they want for the conversion of sinners." Jacinta had been so deeply moved by the vision of hell during the apparition of July 13 that no mortification seemed too great to save sinners.

Bodily Mortifications of Francisco, Jacinta, and Lucia

On September 13, 1917, the fifth apparition took place. The children had been offering various sacrifices. Our Lady told them, "God is pleased with your sacrifices, but He does not want you to sleep with the (penitential) cord on; only wear it during the day-time." On the day after Francisco's death, April 4th, 1919, Our Lady told Jacinta she was to be taken to two different hospitals "not to be cured, but to suffer more for sinners" and that "she was to die all alone far away from home." Her death took place on February 20, 1920 after unbelievable suffering. Can we imagine the anxiety that could smother a person knowing in advance they would suffer greatly and would die all alone? Can we imagine how a child of age ten like Jacinta would feel and what her thoughts would be?

Heroic Suffering

The word *heroic* best describes the acts of penance and sacrifice the children performed in reply to the Angel's and Our Lady's requests. The Angel had knelt with his forehead touching the ground as he prayed during the third Angelic apparition in late September or early October, 1916. Instead of playing their usual games the shepherds prayed while their flocks were pastured. With their foreheads on the ground they prayed for hours and hours, "My God, I believe. I adore. I hope and I love You. I Ask pardon for those who do not believe, do not adore, do not hope and do not love you" — as taught by the Angel. The third time the Angel appeared to them he was holding a chalice in his left hand with the Host suspended above it with some drops of blood falling into the chalice. Leaving the chalice suspended in the air, the Angel knelt down bedside them and made them repeat three times these words: "Most Holy Trinity, Father, Son, and Holy Spirit, I offer You the most precious Body, Blood, Soul, and Divinity of Jesus Christ present in all the tabernacles of the world, in reparation for the sacrileges, outrages, and indifference by which He Himself is offended. And through the infinite merits of His most Sacred Heart, and the Immaculate Heart of Mary, I beg of You the conversion of poor sinners. Make reparation for their crimes, and console your God." The three seers remained in the praying position, heads touching the ground, until it started to turn dark. Francisco and Jacinta spent many hours praying in this manner.

Sister Lucia writes, "From this moment on (Summer of 1916), we had begun to offer to the Lord everything that mortified us, but without looking to impose particular penances on ourselves except to pass entire hours prostrated on the ground — sometimes to the point of exhaustion. Francisco was the first to feel the strain of the prostrate position and would have to remain sitting or kneeling, waiting for Jacinta and me to finish. Francisco said he was not 'able to stay like that for a long time like us' because his back ached so much he just couldn't do it."

During the questioning by the city administrators, who were opposed to the children and crowds going to the place of apparitions, the children were threatened with being boiled alive in oil. They were persecuted by the authorities as were their parents. They were ridiculed by some townfolks. Lucia was particularly persecuted by her own parents who were embarrassed by the claims of the children.

The children squeezed nettles in their hands for penance and pounded them on their legs to offer God yet "another sacrifice." They tied cords around the waist which caused them terrible suffering to the point of tears. When Lucia urged Jacinta to remove her cord when Jacinta was crying from pain Jacinta said, "No, I want to offer this sacrifice to Our Lord in reparation, and for the conversion of sinners." Lucia writes that Jacinta took this matter of making sacrifices for the conversion of sinners so much to heart that she never let a single opportunity escape her. "There were two families in Moita whose children would go around begging for food from door to door. We met them one day as we were going along with our sheep. As soon as we saw them, Jacinta said we should give our lunch to those poor children for the conversion of sinners. She ran to take it to them. That afternoon she told me she was hungry. There were holm oak and oak trees nearby but the acorns on the oaks were still green. I told her we could still eat them. Francisco climbed up a holm oak to fill his pockets but Jacinta told us that we should eat the bitter ones from the oaks instead so we could offer it in sacrifice for sinners She said it was because they were bitter that she wanted to eat them as an offering for sinners."

Lucia writes that the poor children from Moita learned to wait where they expected the shepherd children to pass by and they would accept their lunches. "Jacinta would spot them waiting and run to them with our lunches giving them all the food we were to have for the long day with the sheep, as happy as if we would have all the food we needed. She couldn't wait to give our food away to the children. One particularly hot day in that arid place we thought everything would burn up. We were parched with thirst and there wasn't a drop of water for us to drink. At first we offered the sacrifice of our thirst for sinners but after the mid-day we could hold out no longer. There was a house nearby and I went to ask for some water. The lady gave me a pitcher of water and some bread.... I ran to my companions to share the bread and water and offered the pitcher to Francisco to take a drink. He said he didn't want to. I offered Jacinta some water and she said she wanted to suffer for sinners too so I put the water into the hollow of a rock for the sheep to drink."

Lucia said that Jacinta was really feeling very ill by then with a terrible headache. "The heat was getting worse. Even the shrill singing of the crickets and grasshoppers along with the croaking of the frogs in the nearby pond made Jacinta's suffering almost unbearable. But Jacinta, frail as she was and weakened still more by the lack of food and drink, said to me with the simplicity that was natural for her, 'Tell the crickets and frogs to keep quiet. I have such a terrible headache.' Francisco asked her if she didn't want to suffer for sinners and she replied while holding her head between her hands, 'Yes, I do. Let them sing.'" The children learned well their lessons from the Angel and Our Lady.

Offering of Suffering

Chapter Five

Third Part of the Secret of Fatima Confirms the Need for Sacrifice and Prayer for Souls

In June, 2000 the Holy Father gave permission for the public release of the mysterious third part of the secret which Catholics had anxiously awaited in 1960. The expectations of many were that announcement would be made of some catastrophic incident of worldwide concern like a severe chastisement, etc. Sister Lucia, one of the seers, at age ninety, refused to give her interpretation of the so-called third part of the secret given by Our Lady in 1917.

This author is grateful that the secret was made known at a time when it could be included in this book. The reason to include it as part of this appeal for the sick to offer their sufferings is that Cardinal Ratzinger's interpretation, given below, reinforces the request of the the Blessed Virgin Mary and the Angel in 1917 for sacrifice, reparation, and prayer for the conversion of sinners. In other words, the Church recognizes the holiness of Francisco and Jacinta and goes even further to recognize that the essence of the purpose of the apparitions was for mankind to see the need for sacrifice and penance for its sins and for prayer for the conversion of souls. This aspect of Fatima seems to have been seriously neglected for the past seventy years or so. The Holy Father apparently feels that in spite of the obvious help from Our Lady in the collapse of Communism after the consecration by the Bishops and the Pope of Russia to her Immaculate Heart, the world is far from being secure until it goes through a massive conversion. The sick and dying can make a great contribution to this peace plan of Jesus and Mary with their prayers and suffering.

Great weight should be given to these words of Cardinal Joseph Ratzinger as they relate to the suffering of the faithful in this new century because he is the Prefect of the Congregation for the Doctrine of the Faith. As such he safeguards the doctrine, dogmas, and teachings of the Church. It is a very significant action on his part to take the time to give an interpretation of the secret given to the seers of Fatima.

The following includes the first and second parts of the secret, followed by the third part, all written by Sister Lucia. Following the third part is "An Attempt to Interpret the Secret of Fatima" by Cardinal Ratzinger as released by the Vatican in June, 2000. All three parts speak of the need to pray for the conversion of souls:

> The first part is the vision of Hell. Our Lady showed us a great sea of fire which seemed to be under the earth. Plunged in this fire were demons and souls in human form, like transparent burning embers, all blackened or burnished bronze, floating about in a conflagration, now raised into the air by the flames that issued from within themselves together with great clouds of smoke, now falling back on every side like sparks in a huge fire, without weight or equilibrium, and amid shrieks and groans of pain and despair, which horrified us and made us tremble with fear. The demons could be distinguished by their terrifying and repulsive likeness to frightful and unknown animals, all black and transparent. This vision lasted but an instant. How can we ever be grateful enough to our kind Heavenly Mother, who had already prepared us by promising, in the first Apparition, to take us to Heaven. Otherwise, I think we would have died of fear and terror.
>
> We looked up at Our Lady, who said to us so kindly and so sadly, "You have seen Hell where the souls of

poor sinners go. To save them, God wishes to establish in the world devotion to my Immaculate Heart. If what I say to you is done, many souls will be saved and there will be peace. The war (WW I) is going to end. But if people do not stop offending God, a worse one (WW II) will break out during the Pontificate of Pius XI. When you see a night illumined by an unknown light, know that this is the great sign given you by God that He is about to punish the world for its crimes, by means of war, famine, and persecutions of the Church and of the Holy Father. To prevent this, I shall come to ask for the consecration of Russia to my Immaculate Heart, and Communion of reparation on the First Saturdays. If my requests are heeded, Russia will be converted, and there will be peace. If not, she will spread her errors throughout the world, causing wars and persecution of the Church. The good will be martyred, the Holy Father will have much to suffer; various nations will be annihilated. In the end, my Immaculate Heart will triumph. The Holy Father will consecrate Russia to me, and she will be converted, and a period of peace will be granted to the world."

Third Part:

After the two parts which I have already explained, at the left of Our Lady and a little above, we saw an Angel with a flaming sword in his left hand, flashing. It gave out flames that looked as though they would set the world on fire, but they died out in contact with the splendor that Our Lady radiated towards him from her right hand. Pointing to the earth with his right hand, the Angel cried out in a loud voice, *"Penance. Penance. Penance."* And we saw in an immense light that is God, something similar to how people appear in a mirror when they pass in front of it, a Bishop dressed in white. We had the impression it was the Holy Father. Other bishops, priests, men and women Religious were going up a steep mountain, at the top of which there was a big cross of rough-hewn wood trunks as of a cork tree with bark. Before reaching there the Holy Father passed through a big city half in ruins, and half trembling with halting step, afflicted with pain and sorrow, he prayed for the souls of the corpses he met on the way. Having reached the top of the mountain, and on his knees at the foot of the big cross he was killed by a group of soldiers who fired bullets and arrows at him, and in the same way there died one after another, the other bishops, priests, men and women religious, and various lay people of different ranks and positions. Beneath the two arms of the cross there were two Angels each with a crystal aspersorium in his hand, in which they gathered up the blood of the martyrs and with it, sprinkled the souls that were making their way to God.

An Attempt to Interpret the "Secret" of Fatima by Joseph Card. Ratzinger: (emphasis by this author)

The first and second parts of the "secret" of Fatima have already been so amply discussed in the relative literature that there is no need to deal with them again here. I would just like to recall briefly the most significant point. For one terrible moment, the children were given a vision of Hell. They saw the fall of "the souls of poor sinners." And now they are told why they have been exposed to this moment: "in order to save souls" — to show the way to salvation, The words of the First Letter of Peter come to mind:

As the outcome of your faith you obtain the salvation of your souls (1:9).

To reach this goal, the way indicated — surprisingly for people from the Anglo-Saxon and German cultural world — is devotion to the Immaculate Heart of Mary. A brief comment may suffice to explain this in biblical language. The "heart" indicates the center of human life, the point where reason, will, temperament, and sensitivity converge, where the person finds his unity and his interior orientation. According to Matthew 5:8, the immaculate heart is a heart which, with God's grace, has come to perfect interior unity and therefore "sees God." To be devoted to the Immaculate Heart of Mary means therefore to embrace this attitude of heart, which makes the *fiat* "Your will be done" the defining center of one's whole life. It might be objected that we should not place a human being between ourselves and Christ. But then we remember that Paul did not hesitate to say to his communities: "Imitate me" (1 Cor 4:16, Phil 3:17, 1 Th 1:6, 2 Th 3:7, 9). In the Apostle they could see concretely what it meant to follow Christ. But from whom might we better learn in every age than from the Mother of the Lord?

Thus we come finally to the third part of the "secret" of Fatima which for the first time is being published in its entirety. As is clear from the documentation presented here, the interpretation offered by Cardinal Sodano in his statement of 13 May was first put personally to Sister Lucia. Sister Lucia responded by pointing out that she had received the vision but not its interpretation. The interpretation, she said, belonged not to the visionary but to the Church. After reading the text, however, she said that this interpretation corresponded to what she had experienced and that on her part she thought the interpretation correct. In what follows, therefore, we can only attempt to provide a deeper foundation for this interpretation, on the basis of the criteria already considered.

"To save souls" has emerged as the key word of the first and second parts of the "secret," and the key word of this third part is the threefold cry, "Penance, Penance, Penance!" The beginning of the Gospel comes to mind: "Repent and believe the good news." (Mk 1:5). To understand the signs of the times means to accept the urgency of penance — of conversion — of faith. This is the correct response to this moment of history, characterized by the grave perils outlined in the images that follow. Allow me to add here a personal recollection: in a conversation with me Sister Lucia said that it appeared ever more clearly to her that the purpose of all the apparitions was to help people to grow more and more in their faith, hope, and love — everything else was intended to lead to this.

Let us examine more closely the single images. The angel with the flaming sword on the left of the Mother of God recalls similar images in the Book of Revelation. This represents the threat of judgment which looms all over the world. Today the prospect that the world might be reduced to ashes by a sea of fire no longer seems pure fantasy: man himself, with his inventions, has forged the flaming sword. The vision then shows the power which stands opposed to the force of destruction — the splendor of the Mother of God and, stemming from this in a certain way, the summons to penance. In this way, the importance of human freedom is underlined: the future is not in fact unchangeably set, and the image which the children saw is in no way a film preview of the future in which nothing can be changed.

Indeed, the whole point of the vision is to bring freedom on to the scene and to steer freedom into a positive direction. The purpose of the vision is not to show a film of an irrevocably fixed future. Its meaning is exactly the opposite: it is meant to mobilize the forces of change in the right direction. Therefore we must totally discount fatalistic explanations of the "secret," such as, for example, the claim that the would-be assassin of 13 May, 1981, was merely an instrument of the divine plan guided by Providence and could not therefore, have acted freely, or other similar ideas in circulation. Rather, the vision speaks of dangers and how we might be saved from them.

The next phrases of the text show very clearly once again the symbolic character of the vision. God remains immeasurable, and is the light which surpasses every vision of ours. Human persons appear as in a mirror. We must always keep in mind the limits of the vision itself, which here are indicated visually. The future appears only "in a mirror dimly" (1 Cor 13:12). Let us now consider the individual images which follow in the text of the "secret." The place of the action is described in three symbols: a steep mountain, a great city reduced to ruins, and finally a rough-hewn cross. The mountain and city symbolize the arena of human history: history as an arduous ascent to the summit, history as the arena of human creativity and social harmony, but at the same time, a place of destruction, where man actually destroys the fruits of his own work. The city can be the place of communion and progress, but also of danger and the most extreme menace. The cross transforms destruction into salvation; it stands as a sign of history's misery but also as a promise for history.

At this point human persons appear: the bishop dressed in White ("we had the impression that it was the Holy Father"), other bishops, priests, men and women Religious, and men and women of different ranks and social positions. The Pope seems to precede the others, trembling and suffering because of all the horrors around him. Not only do the houses of the city lie half in ruins, but he makes his way among the corpses of the dead. The Church's path is thus described as a *Via Crucis,* as a journey through a time of violence, destruction and persecution. The history of an entire century can be seen represented in this image. Just as the places of the earth are synthetically described in the two images of the mountain and the city, and are directed towards the cross, so too, time is presented in a compressed way…. In the vision we can recognize the last century of the World Wars and the many local wars which filled the last fifty years and have inflicted unprecedented forms of cruelty. In the "mirror" of this vision we see passing before us the witnesses of the faith decade by decade. Here it would be appropriate to mention a phrase from the letter which Sister Lucia wrote to the Holy Father on 12 May, 1982: "The third part of the 'secret' refers to Our Lady's words, '…if not, (Russia) will spread her errors throughout the world, causing wars and persecutions of the Church. The good will be martyred, the Holy Father will have much to suffer, various nations will be annihilated.'"

In the *Via Crucis* of an entire century, the figure of the Pope has a special role. In his arduous ascent of the mountain we can undoubtedly see a convergence of different Popes. Beginning from Pius X up to the present Pope, they all shared the sufferings of the century and strove to go forward through all the anguish along the path which leads to the Cross. In the vision, the Pope too is killed along with the martyrs. When, after the attempted assassination on May 13, 1981, the Holy Father had the text of the third part of the "secret" brought to him. Was it not inevitable that he should see in it his own fate? He had been very close to death, and he himself explained his survival in the following words, "…it was a mother's hand that guided the bullet's path and in his throes the Pope halted at the threshold of death" (13 May, 1994). That here "a mother's hand" had deflected the fateful bullet only shows once more that there is no immutable destiny, that faith and prayer are forces which can influence history and that in the end prayer is more powerful than bullets and more powerful than armies.

The concluding part of the "secret" uses images which Lucia may have seen in devotional books and which draw their inspiration from long-standing intuitions of faith. It is a consoling vision, which seeks to open a history of blood and tears to the healing power of God. Beneath the arms of the cross, angels gather up the blood of the martyrs, and with it they give life to the souls making their way to God. Here, the blood of Christ and the blood of the martyrs are considered as one: the blood of the martyrs runs down from the arms of the cross. *The martyrs die in common with the Passion of Christ, and their death becomes one with His. "For the sake of the Body of Christ, they complete what is still lacking in His afflictions" (Col 1:24).* Their life has itself become a Eucharist, part of the mystery of the grain of wheat which in dying yields abundant fruit. The blood of the martyrs is the seed of Christians, said Tertullian. As from Christ's death, from His wounded side, the Church was born, so the death of the witnesses is fruitful for the future life of the Church. Therefore, the vision of the third part of the "secret," so distressing at first, concludes with an image of hope: *no suffering is in vain, and it is a suffering Church, a Church of martyrs, which becomes a sign-post for man in his search for God.* The loving arms of God welcome not only those who suffer like Lazarus, who found great solace there and mysteriously represents Christ, who wished to become for us the poor Lazarus. *There is something more: from the suffering of the witnesses there come a purifying and renewing power, because their suffering is the actualization of the suffering of Christ Himself and a communication in the here and now of its saving effect.*

And so we come to the final question. What is the meaning of the "secret" of Fatima as a whole (in its three parts)? What does it say to us? First of all we must affirm with Cardinal Sodano: "...the events to which the third part of the 'secret' of Fatima refers now seem part of the past." Insofar as individual events are described, they belong to the past. Those who expected exciting apocalyptic revelations about the end of the world or the future course of history are bound to be disappointed. Fatima does not satisfy our curiosity in this way, just as Christian faith in general cannot be reduced to an object of mere curiosity. *What remains was already evident when we began our reflections on the text of the "secret:" the exhortation to prayer as the path of "salvation for souls" and, likewise, the summons to penance and conversion.*

I would like to mention another key expression of the "secret" which has become justly famous — "my Immaculate Heart will triumph." What does this mean? The heart open to God, purified by contemplation of God, is stronger than guns and weapons of every kind. The Fiat of Mary, the word of her Heart, has changed the history of the world, because it brought the Savior into the world — because, thanks to her *Yes,* God could become man in our world and remains so for all time. The Evil One has power in this world, as we see and experience continually. He has power because our freedom continually lets itself be led away from God. but since God Himself took a human heart and has thus steered human freedom towards what is good, the freedom to choose evil no longer has the last word. From that time forth, the word that prevails is this: "In this world you will have tribulation, but take heart; I have overcome the world." (Jn 16:33). The message of Fatima invites us to trust in this promise.

— Joseph Cardinal Ratzinger
Prefect of the Congregation
for the Doctrine of the Faith

Chapter Six

The Suffering of St. Therese of Lisieux, Doctor of the Church

St. Therese of the Child Jesus and of the Holy Face (The Little Flower) died at the age of 24 in 1897. Almost all of her years were spent in some form of suffering, but her last eighteen months were a veritable agony of body and especially the soul. She was a happy child until her mother died when Therese was four and a half years old. Her older sister Pauline became her "mother" but entered the convent of the Lisieux Carmel of the Discalced Carmelites. This broke her heart. Marie, another sister became her "mother" but she too entered the Carmel leaving Therese inconsolable.

At age ten she became ill with a very mysterious illness and came near losing her life. She was exceptionally sensitive and cried almost constantly over almost everything. She came to hate her weakness in that regard but she was from the earliest age very spiritual and very holy. In the convent, at age 22 she became very ill with tuberculosis and coughed up blood in April, 1896. About two days after this experience she entered into a trial of her faith that lasted up until the very last moments of her life. Literally, she was only two or three minutes from dying when she finally showed signs of relief from this trial and died in a state of ecstasy. She suffered terribly from the cold winters of France in the damp cold of Normandy. She received no consolations, no visions, no signs that she was God's special child and yet in the year 1925 she was canonized, and called the greatest modern saint of the Church. In 1997 she was declared a Doctor of the Church because of holiness and her "little way."

There was one thing that stood out in her writings and conversations with her sisters in the convent — and that was her special love of suffering. Could her writings have an important message for us on the subject of suffering and how suffering can save souls? Let's take into consideration what the Church sets as a criteria for one to be a Doctor of the Church. And further, consider that she is only one of three women so designated by the Church. And what company she is in! With St. Teresa of Avila and St. Catherine of Siena she is looked upon as one with a worthy message for the whole Church. Of all the thousands of canonized saints of the Church only thirty-two are doctors, including the three women. The three major requirements for one to be declared a Doctor are 1). Holiness that is truly outstanding even among saints, 2). *To be known for a depth of doctrinal content,* and 3). *An extensive body of writings that the Church can recommend to its members as free from error and faithful to her authentic tradition.*

We will try to limit our discussion on Therese to her life as it reflects the depth of her suffering, its forms, and her thoughts on suffering. Considering the criteria above, we should give much weight to her comments on suffering and its benefits. One Pope said that St. Therese had found the secret to sanctity. Suffering played a major role in her holy life — suffering in soul and body.

Suffering as a Novice

As a young novice of age fifteen, Therese had to adjust to the chores assigned her. She had no similar responsibilities at home and was very awkward in accomplishing her housecleaning chores, bringing severe and frequent criticism from Mother Marie de Gonzague, the Mother Superior. It was strange that Mother Marie treated Therese coldly and remained at a "distance" from her, yet she was the first in the convent to recognize the basic holiness of the novice. Later, she would say about Therese that she could have been an effective superior of a convent at age 23 or 24. Mother

Marie detected the extraordinary wisdom of Therese and wrote of her after Therese's death that she was indeed a very holy nun with unusual spiritual maturity.

Therese had great sensitivity to the winter cold and said herself that "I felt cold enough to die." And this from one who never complained to anyone about anything, even when she was still doing her assignments and was literally dying of tuberculosis. She would not ask for an extra blanket although she could have. She wasn't relieved of her duties until five months before her death on September 30, 1897.

One of her greatest sufferings was over the strokes that affected her father Louis's mind. He was placed in an institution for the mentally ill and was seriously ill for over three years while Therese was in the convent and could do nothing but pray for him. Later she would say that her only comfort was to offer her suffering over him for sinners. If he had died, her cross would not have been as heavy as to see him in his condition and not be able to help him. Only if one knew of the great love that existed between Louis and his "Queen" could they understand her grief over his condition.

It was apparently the will of God that the doctor assigned to care for the nuns had misdiagnosed her illness — shortness of breath, wheezing in the lungs, and finally coughing up of blood on the night of April 3-4, 1896. By then it was too late to help her condition. She went improperly diagnosed until only a few months before her death.

Only a few days after the coughing up of blood she entered into the "thickest darkness," her trial of faith. She was constantly tempted to believe there was nothing after death but a dark void and that heaven did not exit. She fought heroically against this temptation that was so violent she resorted to writing the Credo in her own blood on paper and carried the paper near her heart until she died. Her illness at age ten was considered by her and others to have been caused by the evil one. She said, "I became so early in life the spouse of Jesus, it was necessary for me to suffer from my very infancy." And, "Since my First Communion, when I begged Jesus to change for me all earthly consolations into bitterness, I always had a desire to suffer."

She spent almost a year with a wet-nurse so she could regain her health in her very first year of life. She had many bouts with lung congestion and her mother spoke of the wheezing she heard in Therese's chest after walking rapidly. In 1877 her Mother writes, "My little Therese is ill, and I am anxious. She is always having colds and then gets congested."

In the elementary grades at the Benedictine Abbey, she was often seen in tears, because, a teacher said, "Therese understood how much venial sin offends the good God."

After the coughing episode and the start of her dry spell of faith she found no spiritual consolation or relief from temptations against her faith, not until the very day of her death. Sister Marie of the Trinity, her former novice, had this to say at the process for canonization, "One day she was speaking to me about the temptations against faith she was suffering. I said to her, very much surprised, 'But those beautiful poems that you are composing are giving the lie to what you're telling me.' She answered: 'I sing of what I want to believe, but it is without any feeling. I would not even want to tell you the degree of blackness the night is in my soul for fear of making you share in my temptations.'"

"Ah! Above All, I Long To Be a Martyr"
— St. Therese of Lisieux

"Martyrdom! It was a dream of my childhood and it has grown up with me in my little cell of Carmel." She also wrote," I am quite content to be ill all of my life if that gives pleasure to God, and I am even willing that my life should be very long. The only grace I ask is that I may die of love." With regard to her physical suffering Therese told her sister, Mother Agnes, in August, just a month before she died, "Oh, if one only knew." And in September: "O Mother, it's very easy to write beautiful things about suffering, but writing is nothing … nothing. One must suffer so in order to know." In her yellow notebook she wrote *"Never would I have believed it was possible to suffer so much! Never! Never! I cannot explain this except by the ardent desires I have to save souls."* These words were spoken on September 30, just a few hours before her death. (Therese was not given any injections of morphine through all of her sufferings of the last eighteen months, because Mother de Gonzague would not permit it.)

A Profound Change

There came a time in 1893 when Therese made a profound change in her thoughts about suffering. As stated above, she had a desire to suffer. Now she had not a desire for suffering *but a love of suffering*. This point has been seldom written of but is very significant. It did not escape Abbey Andre Combes who wrote of this change in Therese in his book *St. Therese and Suffering*. The basis for this change was still the proof of her love for Jesus and the conversion of souls. It was the fulfillment of her spiritual development. *It was her desire to completely fulfill the will of God in everything, transcending even the desire for suffering.*

The Value Therese Placed on Suffering

In October, 1888 Therese wrote Celine, "Remember that if God gave us the whole universe with all the treasures it contains, it could not be compared to the very lightest suffering." She called it the "great grace" the day her Father entered the mental institution at Caen. Her reasoning, probably well over the heads of those not tuned to the value of suffering, was: "Later on in heaven, it will be our delight to look back upon those dark days of our exile. Yes, the three years of our dear father's martyrdom seem to me the richest and the most fruitful of our lives. I would not exchange them for the most sublime ecstasies; and my heart, conscious of this valuable gift, cries out in gratitude: 'Blessed be Thou, O my God, for the graces of those years that we have passed in misfortune.'" To her sister, Mother Agnes: "O my dear Mother, though our cross was bitter, how precious and sweet it was, for from our hearts came nothing but aspirations of love and gratitude! No longer did we walk, we ran, we flew in the paths of perfection."

And Abbe Combes says that "heavy or light, suffering is always a mark of God's love: He gives the Cross only to His chosen friends." In her autobiography Therese writes, "When a man wants to reach an end, he must take the necessary means. Now that Jesus has made me understand that He would give me souls through the Cross, the more the Cross fell to my lot, the more my attraction to suffering increased. For five years this way was mine, but I alone knew it. This was the very flower I wanted to offer Jesus, a hidden flower which would breathe out its perfume only in heaven."

At age 16, in a letter to Celine on March 12, 1889, Therese writes from the Carmel, "...We must offer our sufferings to Jesus to save souls. Poor souls! They have fewer graces than we have and yet Our Lord shed all His Blood for their salvation and He wills that their eternal happiness should depend upon a single aspiration of our hearts. How wonderful a mystery! If one sigh can save a soul, how many souls may be saved by sufferings like ours! Let us refuse nothing to Jesus."

Abbe Combes: "Grace now teaches her to penetrate more deeply into the mystery of suffering. Her soul is enlightened and grows in love and confidence. Not only is the Cross now to be desired for its intrinsic value, whatever the pain that accompanies it, but it is a privilege, a happiness, and a joy. It is a privilege, because man alone can suffer as did Jesus, with Him and for the same ends. Angels, pure spirits in the enjoyment of the eternal beatitude, are unable to suffer, and envy men their privilege.

"It is a happiness, because, being in accordance with the order of salvation and the adorable will of God, it brings man into union with the wisdom of God and the designs of His infinite mercy.

"It is the highest joy, for it is the triumph of grace that nature should find its highest perfection in that which mortifies it. It is the highest joy when at length the soul finds nothing so sweet and attractive as to do the Will of the Father even when it brings it to crucifixion and death.

"The solution of the theoretical problem and of the practical difficulties aroused by the various sufferings of mankind, not excluding the greatest of all, death, *is to take delight in them as in so many proofs of love."*

"...Boldly she (Therese) inverts the natural relationship of men and angels and considers that man has the advantage in being able to suffer. This original idea, based on sound philosophical and theological grounds, inspired this child of genius with some of her best verses." Therese proceeds in her wisdom concerning suffering, when she advances to the point where she decides that *doing the complete Will of God in all things* is even more sublime than is suffering alone. It would include suffering, of course, yet it might exclude it as well, and provide a different form of the cross! If God sends the Cross to Therese, she loves it and does not ask to be delivered from it. He sends her joy, a life without pain, a foretaste of heaven. This, too, she loves as a gift from God and as powerful a means for saving souls as is suffering, *if she receives it with equal love."*

There is a very interesting difference between what St. John of the Cross believed about the soul that reaches the final stage of union with God, and what Therese experiences in the same stage of unity. St. John of the Cross says that in that condition the soul is beyond the reach of trials; no more suffering or afflictions, no more aridity; now there is only happiness and glory. St. John seems to say that the soul is then free from all darkness and even suffering, and that any trial seems to be incompatible with the union of trans-formation in the last stage of contemplation. But Therese's doctrine of complete self-abandonment to God allows for *anything* to happen to the soul in that state — where the highest action of the soul consists in the fullest self-surrender to the free action of God's Will. "Therese believes that God was pleased with her sufferings, but now she understands that her *complete renunciation of self* would please Him more.... She is now at the complete disposal of the merciful love of her Creator."

Abbey Combes says that "In Therese's act of self-oblation she offered herself without reserve by an act of purest love. But if she had given herself up to Him, He in return seemed to have given her up. Despite one or two remarkable consolations, the almost unbroken rule was that she received no sign of protection, or of tenderness either for soul or body. The forces of dissolution and death, of temptation and darkness, were unchecked." An example of her physical tortures: Mother Agnes at the Apostolic process said, "She (Therese) had become so emaciated that in several places the bones had worked their way through her skin, and two most painful wounds had been formed." Although Dr. La Neele told Mother de Gonzague that Therese should be seen by a doctor every day, she was permitted to see one only three times in a five week period. And Mother de Gonzague would not permit the use of morphine.

Sister Genevieve, at the Apostolic process said, "She (Therese) admitted that when she prayed heaven to come to her help, it was then that she felt the least help of all. When we expressed our surprise, she replied, 'But I am not in the least discouraged. I turn to God and to all the saints, and I thank them all the same. It seems to me that they want to see to what lengths I shall carry my trust. No! It is not for nothing that I have taken to my heart the words of Job: Even though God should kill me, yet I would trust in Him.'"

St. Therese said, "The day will come when shadows will disappear; then nothing will remain save joy and delight." We can look forward to such a reward ourselves when we offer our suffering "which has been accepted with humility, borne with utter self-abandonment to God, and transfigured by love."

St. Therese's Words on Suffering in Peace

"I confess that this word *peace* seemed rather strong but, the other day, reflecting on it, I found the secret of being able to suffer in peace. To say that we suffer in peace does not mean that we suffer with joy, at least with a joy that is felt. In order to suffer in peace, it is enough to will truly all that Jesus wills."

The Meaning of Suffering With Joy
— Fr. Francois Jamart, O.C.D.
Author of *Complete Spiritual Doctrine of St. Therese of Lisieux*

Suffering with joy means to transcend the bitterness we naturally experience so that we place all our contentment in pleasing God Who sends us suffering; to place our happiness in sacrificing ourselves for Jesus and in imitation of Jesus, in spite of our natural repugnance for it. This is the joy that surpasses all joy, a joy in which all creatures — which are truly nothing — give place to the Uncreated who is reality. How was Therese able to derive such happiness from what is so repugnant to our nature? She herself tells us: "It is impossible to create such sentiments in ourselves. It is the Holy Ghost who imparts them to us."

From Fr. Jamart, OCD

If St. Therese of the Child Jesus desired sufferings, it was because they were a means of corresponding to God's designs. "Jesus made me understand that it is by the cross that he would give me souls, and my attraction for suffering grew in the same measure that my sufferings increased." But she never asked Him to send her greater ones, and she gives us the reason for it: "I never want to ask God for greater sufferings, for these, then, would be *my* sufferings. I would have to bear them alone and I have never succeeded in doing anything unaided."

If we accept the sacrifices God sends us, and are faithful in bearing the crosses each day, God, if He judges it good, can, in His love, give us heavier ones. In the meantime, let us simply offer to suffer everything that will please Him. He will, thus, be free to grant us the sacrifices of His own choice.

Therese understood, as few souls have done, the greatness and effectiveness of suffering. Being pre-eminently God's gift to men, it is also, at least after abandonment to God, the best proof we can give of our love for God. More than any other work, it sanctifies us and increases our capacity for happiness and our measure of glory. More than any other, it is the instrument of the salvation of souls. For it serves to identify us with the suffering of Christ and makes us His co-workers in the plan of redemption.

Like Therese, let us then give to suffering the welcome it deserves. "When we suffer out of love and to prove our love," says Fr. Combes, "we shall also die through love and to prove our love." To die is then a most happy event. And since it is the last thing we experience here below, every suffering prepares us for it and the total of all our immolated joys becomes the most beautiful offering that can be presented by us to the divine Crucified.

Therese's Words on Suffering

Jesus wishes to bring His kingdom to souls more by suffering than by brilliant preaching.

Trials help greatly to detach us from earth. They make us look to God, rather than to this world.

The martyrdom of the heart is no less fruitful than the shedding of blood.

It is so consoling to think that Jesus, Divine Strength itself, has experienced our weakness, that he trembled at the sight of the bitter chalice which He had so ardently desired.

My joy is to love suffering. I smile in the midst of tears and receive with thanksgiving the thorns as well as the flowers.

Jesus has always treated me as a favorite child. It is true that His Cross has accompanied me from childhood, but He has made me love this Cross passionately.

Willingly would I remain all my religious life in this dark tunnel of spiritual dryness into which Jesus has led me. I wish only that my darkness may obtain light for sinners.

Do you know what days are my Sundays and feast days? They are the days when the good God tries me the most.

Nothing is too great to suffer in order to win the palm of eternal life.

I value sacrifice more than ecstasy. I find my happiness in suffering, as I find it nowhere else.

Jesus gives me just what I can bear at the moment, no more; and if in a moment He increases my suffering, He also increase my strength.

"You have many trials today," someone said to St. Therese. "Yes, but I love them. I love everything that the dear God gives to me."

If I did not suffer from moment to moment, I would not be able to keep patience, but I see only the present moment. I forget the past and take care not to peep into the future.

Jesus wants to take complete possession of your heart. That is why He makes you suffer much, but Oh what joy will your soul know at the moment of your entrance into heaven.

Suffering united to love is the one thing we should desire in this valley of tears.

O Guardian Angel, fly in my stead to those who are dear to me, dry their tears; tell them of the goodness of Jesus and of the benefit of suffering and Oh so softly murmur my name.

Fortunately I did not ask for suffering. If I had asked for it, I fear I wouldn't have the patience to bear it. Whereas, if it is coming directly from God's will, He cannot refuse to give me the patience and the grace to bear it.

I was saying to God that all the prayers offered for me were not to assuage my sufferings but to help sinners.

August 16, 1897 — Therese is on her death bed, six weeks before her death:

Sister Genevieve (Celine, her blood sister) writes: "When I rose early this morning, I found my dear little sister (Therese), pale and disfigured by suffering and anguish. She said, 'The devil is around me; I don't see him but I feel him. He is tormenting me; he is holding me with an iron hand to prevent me from taking the slightest relief; he is increasing my pains in order to make me despair. And I can longer pray! I can only look at the Blessed Virgin (statue) and say *Jesus.* How necessary is that prayer at Compline — *deliver us from the phantoms of the night.*

"'I experience something mysterious. Until now, I've suffered especially in my right side, but God asked me if I wanted to suffer for you, and I immediately answered that I did. At the same instant, my left side was seized with an incredible pain. I'm suffering for you and the devil doesn't want it.' Deeply moved, I lighted a blessed candle and calm was restored shortly afterward, without, however, her new physical suffering being taken away from her. Since then she called her right side: 'Therese's side,' and her left side, 'Celine's side.'" About 7:20 P. M. on September 30, 1897, Therese died. Her last words were: "Well, all right! All right! Oh! I wouldn't want to suffer less! Oh! I love Him … My God … I … love … You!"

Chapter Seven

The Suffering of Sr. Josefa Menendez, Victim Soul

In this chapter we will discuss a victim soul who was chosen by Jesus Himself to offer suffering for the conversion of souls who were almost certainly going to be lost unless strong prayer and sacrifice were made on their behalf. In Pope John Paul II's Apostolic letter we have shown the reasoning behind the utilization of human suffering for the salvation of souls and will not repeat that information here. St. Paul has shown why this is allowed by God and how he participated in this salvation as he explained how his afflictions "made up that which was lacking, for the body of Christ, that is, the church." (Col 1:24)

The reader may find this reading highly motivating because here Jesus explains almost constantly to Josefa why and how He uses her suffering to save souls. The same would apply to anyone's suffering as far as the how and why are concerned, even if they were not specifically chosen as a victim soul. A caution is presented here: the saints have said that we should not ask to be a victim soul as such; that God will make the choice and He will know that soul who is predisposed to offer themselves in that manner and He will take the initiative, just as he did with Theresa Newman of Germany, Blessed Padre Pio of Italy, and St. Francis of Assisi — all of whom bore the stigmata, his sacred wounds. This does not prevent us from participating in the salvation of souls by volunteering those afflictions and sorrows that are part of our daily life as willed by God.

In the case of Sr. Josefa, Jesus deals with her as the Sacred Heart who seeks her cooperation as a victim soul to suffer for the conversion of sinners. He asks her to consider the sufferings of that Heart and the love that Heart holds for mankind. His primary message for us through her is His Love and Mercy for sinners; that He will forgive and forgive and forgive — so long as a soul is repentant and loves Him. Jesus asks first if she is willing to share in His sufferings. Sr. Josefa's diary revealed the unbelievable suffering she had to undergo to save one soul. Jesus taught her the priceless value of the human soul and how important and critical it is for us to offer penances and sufferings of all kinds as a regular practice in our daily lives, for the salvation of souls.

As you read through His words to her you will find that He gave her a truly unique cross to carry. He permitted Satan to take her spirit in some mysterious manner to hell where she experienced horrible torments feeling as if she herself were a lost soul damned forever. On one occasion she returned from one such visit to hell with her garment smoking and burns on her body which remained and could still be see after her death. She was only thirty-three years old when she died. This experience was repeated many times and is beyond our comprehension as to how this can take place. But His ways are not our ways This information is in the category of Private Revelation and her book carries the Imprimatur of E. Morrogh Bernard, Vicar General, Wesmonasterii, England, May 5, 1953.

Participation In The Sufferings of Christ

Sr. Josefa was a nun of the Society of the Sacred Heart of Jesus in the convent of Les Feuillants in Poitier, France, although Josefa was born in Spain. It might be helpful to begin Josefa's journey of suffering with an explanation about the role of the victim soul as contained in the introduction of her book:

In the new testament a new sacrifice takes the place of the old; Jesus is the sole Mediator, sole priest, sole

Victim, and His sacrifice is no longer symbolic but real and infinite.

If then, Jesus Christ wishes to associate other victims with Himself, he must be closely united to Him, and share His feelings, in order to enter fully into His sacrifice; hence they can only be human beings, endowed with intelligence and will.

He Himself chose these persons, and because they are free He asks them for their voluntary co-operation. Those who accept put themselves at His mercy, and He then makes use of them as by sovereign right.

Assimilated and transformed into Christ, the victim-soul expresses the sentiments of Christ Jesus to God the father, and to Christ Himself. Her attitude is one of humiliation, penance, and expiation, sentiments which ought to animate the souls she represents.

And because of this identification with Christ, the victim-soul shares in His dolorous Passion and undergoes, to a greater or lesser degree, and in various but generally superhuman ways, the torments and agonies that were His.

When the suffering is borne for one specially chosen sinner the victim endures the just retribution due to this sinner for his crimes. Every kind of trial is endured, be it illness or even persecution by the spirits of darkness of which the victim becomes the sport.

With Sister Josefa this was the case to an extraordinary degree. Victim at the express desire of Her Lord, not only was her whole being immolated, but the manner of the immolation itself varied according to the particular attributes of God to which she had sacrificed herself.

Saint Therese of the Child Jesus offered herself as a victim of merciful love; Marie des Vallees, as a victim of God's Justice, Saint Margaret Mary, of both Justice and Mercy, and so it was with Sister Josefa. Christ told her His wishes in even more explicit terms than He had used with Saint Margaret Mary.

"I have chosen you to be a victim of My Heart." "You are the victim of My love." "You are the victim of My love and mercy." "I want you to be the victim of divine justice and the comfort of My Heart."

For all these reasons Josefa must suffer. "You suffer in your soul and body, because you are the victim of My Soul and Body. How could you not suffer in your heart, since I have chosen you as the victim of My Heart?" (19 December, 1920)

As victim of the Heart of Jesus she suffered in order to console the Heart that has been so wounded by the ingratitude of men. As victim of love and mercy she suffered that the merciful love of Jesus might overwhelm with graces the sinner He so loved. As victim of the divine justice she carried the intolerable burden of the divine reproaches, and expiated for guilty souls, who would owe their salvation to her. Her mission exacted perpetual immolation on her part, and our Lord did not hide it from her. "Love, suffer, and obey," He said to her, "so that I may realize My plans in you." (9th January, 1921)

On 12th June, 1923 He corroborated the whole of this plan as it affected her. "As for you, you will live in the most complete and profound obscurity, and as you are My chosen victim, you will suffer, and overwhelmed by suffering you will die. Seek neither rest nor alleviation; you will find none, for such is My will. But My love will sustain you, and never shall I fail you."

But before making her endure such piercing and keen agony, He had asked and obtained her consent; for though He is Sovereign Lord and Master, He nevertheless respects the liberty of the creature.

"Are you willing?..." He said to Josefa, and as she shrank at the prospect before her, He left her. She was heartbroken at His departure, but our Lady came, and suggested to her child: "Do not forget that your love is free." Several times Josefa tried to escape from the path before her, then Jesus left her, and it was only after she had called Him again and again that he came back to receive from her a willing offering of that which He had suggested only as a possibility. Usually she accepted most generously.

"I offered myself to serve Him in any way He might choose." God knew Himself free to act in any way He chose, and he said once again: "I am your God, you belong to Me; of your own free will, you have handed yourself over. From now on you cannot refuse Me anything." (23rd July, 1922). "If you do not deliver yourself up to My will, what can I do?" (21st April, 1922)

She surrendered; like her Master she would be a willing victim … like Him, too, she would be a pure victim. For how can one expiate another's sins, when one has to expiate one's own? From her birth God had enveloped her in purity, for there cannot be found in her life any fault to which she voluntarily consented. Her greatest infidelities, as she herself owned, were a certain reluctance to respond to the call of grace and indecision in the face of a disconcerting mission; nothing therefore that was a stain on her heart and soul.

Many times when He wanted her to re-state that she was His victim He opened the question by conferring on her a grace of still greater purification. "I want you to suffer for me, Josefa, but I will begin by letting the arrow of love which is to purify your soul fall on you, for as My victim, you must be all-pure." (17th June, 1923)

In her pure conscience, on which suffering was about to descend, there was found no taint of sin, and consequently there was no work of expiation to be done, and that was why the fruits of salvation could be transferred to other souls. Her sufferings bore a two-fold character, as is indeed the case with all true victims. As a victim chosen by Christ Himself to continue and complete His redemptive work, she must be very closely united with Christ the Redeemer, and share

His Passion by enduring the self-same sufferings as His own; as an expiatory victim for the sins of others, her pains would be proportionate to the sins of the offender for whom she was atoning.

The Passion of Christ being our sole salvation, if we are to be purified and saved, we must of necessity come into contact with the Blood shed by the Lamb. The great cry of the dying Christ is a pressing invitation to the whole human race to hasten to the savior's fountains from which all graces flow.

This contact with Christ's Blood is immediately secured by souls that answer His appeal. Others, and alas! they are many, voluntarily remain aloof. It is these that Christ will seek to reach through other souls whom he makes use of as channels of His mercies. They are the most fruitful of all the branches of the mystic vine. Loaded with the sap flowing from Christ Himself, and completely one with Him, by their solidarity with the sinner they stand liable for his sins; so being one with him and one with Christ, in them and by them, grace is communicated. They are victim-souls.

How intimate must be their identification with the crucified if they are to carry out their part of the contract fully! Full union with Him is implied, while He on His part imprints on their souls, hearts, and bodies the living image of His sorrowful Passion.

All His sufferings are renewed in them; they will be contradicted, persecuted, humbled, scourged, and crucified; and what man fails to inflict, that God Himself will supply by mysterious pains, agonies, stigmata, which will make of them living crucifixes.

How great must be the power of mediation of such souls! How efficacious their intercession, when they implore divine mercy, pardon and salvation for their brethren; when in them and through them, the Precious Blood of Christ, infinitely more powerful than that of Abel, cries to the Father!

There is this, however, to notice with regard to some saints, notably, Saint Francis of Assisi, that the Passion, as it were, abides in them, God's ultimate plan apparently being to shape them into finished copies of the Crucified. It is God's response to their adoring love of His Passion, and He makes them share both physically and morally in the torments of His Beloved Son.

There is a further purpose with regard to expiatory victims: He seems to dispossess them in favor of other souls, for the Passion of Christ, after marking them with His sign, passes through them, in order to bring about in the sinner for whom they suffer the graces of the sacrifice of Calvary.

They are thus co-redeemers in the full sense of the word; love for their neighbor urges them on, their mission is different from that of others. For whereas God is pleased to allow those other souls of whom we spoke to remain in contemplation of Him, giving glory to His infinite perfections by their love, it is otherwise with victim-souls; when they contemplate Him, He unveils the immensity of His love for souls and the grief with which the loss of sinners fills Him. The sight of this breaks their hearts, and their longing to console Christ is not satisfied with mere words of love; it stirs up their zeal. At whatever price, they will win souls to Him, and He kindles this zeal still more. It is the love of the Sacred Heart Itself, communicated to them, with which they love sinners; love which gives them a superhuman endurance.

Her sufferings took various forms. Jesus wished Josefa to feel the pain of the nails in His hands and feet — the bitterness of sorrow and anguish of His Heart, the pain of His pierced side. On 13 September, 1921, Jesus told her "There is a soul that is grievously wounding Me ... be not afraid if you feel yourself totally abandoned, for I shall make you share the anguish of My Heart. Keep My Cross, until that soul recognizes the truth. Take My Cross, My Nails, My Crown. I go in search of souls." (17th June, 1923). His burning thirst for the salvation of souls urged her to attempt every kind of reparation and expiation within her power. One that she feared greatly was the devil.

God also confounds the pride of the spirit of darkness, who in spite of all his power and rage makes no headway, but meets with constant defeat, which greatly enhances God's glory. So it was with Sister Josefa. The devil tried by every possible means to delude and beguile her, disguising himself as an "angel of light," even going so far as to assume the very features of Jesus Christ Himself. Most often however, he tried to turn her from her chosen path by inflicting on her grievous bodily harm.... Even as a postulant, showers of blows, administered by an invisible fist, fell upon her day and night, especially when she was in prayer and reiterating her determination always to be faithful. At other times she was violently snatched away from the chapel, or prevented from entering it. Again and again the devil appeared to her in the guise of a terrifying dog, snake, or worse still, in human form.

Soon the forcible abductions became more frequent, in spite of the supervision exercised by Superiors. Under their very eyes she suddenly disappeared, and after long search would be found thrown into some loft, or beneath heavy furniture, or in some unfrequented spot. In their presence she was burnt, and without seeing the devil, they saw her clothes consumed and on her body unmistakable traces of fire, which caused wounds that took a long time to heal.

Lastly, there occurred a phenomenon very rare in the lives of the Saint: God permitted the devil to take her down into hell. There she spent long hours, sometimes a whole night, in unspeakable agony. Though she was dragged down into the bottomless pit more than a hundred times each sojourn seemed to her to be the first, and appeared to last countless ages. She endured all the tortures of hell with the one exception of hatred of God. Not the least of these torments was to hear the sterile confessions of the damned, their cries of hatred, of pain, and of despair.

Josefa would be filled with zeal for souls, even after the worst agonies.

Our Lord would show her the treasures of reparation and expiation she had gained by her repeated ordeals and allowed her to witness in hell the devil's outbursts of fury, when there escaped from him souls of whom he thought he had a firm hold, but for whom she was offering expiation. The thought that she could console and rest Our Lord and gain souls for Him kept up her heroic spirit and excited her zeal.

After nights of unspeakable torment, crushed, yet ever gallant, she rose at the hour of the Rule and resumed her ordinary labors, asking no exceptions from common life.

Words of Jesus and the Blessed Virgin Mary To Josefa On Suffering:

Do not be afraid of suffering, for you will always be given sufficient strength to bear it. Think of this; you have only today in which to suffer and love ... eternity will be all joy.

I want you to save souls.... Look at the fire in My heart; it is the craving for them that will burn up yours.

You will gain them by your offerings. Stay still in My Heart and fear nothing.

When I leave you so cold, I am using your warmth to give heat to other souls. When I leave you a prey to anguish, your suffering wards off divine justice when it is about to strike sinners.... When it seems to you as if you did not love Me and yet you tell Me unceasingly that you do, then you console My Heart most.

See what your loving heart does to mine, for though you feel cold and imagine you no longer love Me, it holds back My justice from punishing sinners. One single act of love in the loneliness in which I leave you repairs for many of the acts of ingratitude of which I am the object.

It please, Me to see you famished for My love and burnt with longing to see Me loved. That by itself is consolation to My Heart. Yes, pray for souls for which I have given you charge. A few more sacrifices and they will return to Me.

Listen, I want you to give Me souls. Only love in all you do is required. Suffer because you love, work because you love, and above all abandon yourself to love.... I want to make use of you as a tired man uses a stick to lean on.

Showing Josefa His Heart, Jesus said, "Come and tell Me all you are afraid of. When you feel unable to bear pain, come here! If you are afraid of being humbled, come here! If you are seized with apprehension, come closer still!"

Our Lady told her: "Daughter, you must not worry like this. You know all that Jesus is to you.... Suffer in silence, but without this mental anguish. Love very much but without introspection ... if you fall do not be afflicted above measure. We are both here to raise you up, and I will never forsake you." and.... "If you want to be a comfort to Jesus, I will tell you what gives Him pleasure: you must offer everything you do for souls, without any personal interest whatever, and act solely for the glory of His Heart.

I want you to help Me by your littleness and helplessness to snatch souls from the enemy who wants to devour them.

Our Lady: "Child of my heart, I beg of you not to refuse My Son anything He asks of you. Not your happiness only but that of many depends on your generosity. Many souls will be the gainers by what you endure, so be faithful and abandon yourself wholly. If you but knew the value of a soul!

Be on the lookout today for what costs and mortifies you most, and make as many acts of love as you can. How different souls would be if they knew this secret ... how dead to self they would become and how they would console My Heart.

There are some Christian souls and even very pious ones that are held back from perfection by some attachment. But when another offers Me her actions united to My infinite merits, she obtains grace for them to free themselves and make a fresh start. Many others live in indifference and even in sin, but when helped in the same way, recover grace, and will eventually be saved. Others, again, and these are very numerous, are obstinate in wrongdoing and blinded by error. They would be damned if some faithful soul did not make supplication for them, thus obtaining grace to touch their hearts, but their weakness is so great that they run the risk of a relapse into their sinful life; *these I take away into the next world without any delay, and that is how I save them.* Unite all you do to My actions, whether you work or whether you rest. Unite your breathing to the beating of My Heart. How many souls you would save that way.

Yes, offer yourself to obtain that soul's forgiveness. A soul will profit even after the greatest sins, if she humbles herself. It is pride that provokes my Father's wrath, and it is loathed by Him with an infinite hatred.

The next day, of the soul whose pride wounded Him so grievously, He reminded Josefa, "I want that soul to return to Me as quickly as possible. Are you willing to suffer for her?... Offer everything you do today for that intention."

When a soul does a costly act out of self-interest or to please herself, but not out of love, she gains little merit. On the other hand, a very little thing offered with great love consoles my Heart so much that it inclines towards her, and forgets all her worthlessness. My one desire is to be loved. If souls but knew the excess of My love they would not disregard it ... that is why I go seeking them out and spare nothing to get them to come back to Me. Suffer with Me and never cease to offer My Blood for souls.

Those souls must come back to Me ... Pray hard that they may allow grace to penetrate them.

Our Lady: Do not fear pain and suffering. I wish you could see how many souls have come back to Jesus while you were under temptation.

Do not think that I love you more that I console you, than when I ask you to suffer.

Souls run to perdition, and my Blood is lost for them. But souls that love Me are sacrificing and consuming themselves as victims of reparation, and they draw down God's mercy, and that is what saves the world.

A little group of fervent souls can obtain mercy for many sinners. My Heart cannot resist their prayers.

Josefa: What I have seen gives me great courage to suffer, and makes me understand the value of the smallest sacrifice; Jesus gathers them up and uses them to save souls. It is blindness to avoid pain even in very small things, for not only is it of great worth to ourselves, but it serves to guard many from the torments of hell.

A Special Lesson From Jesus About Saving Souls — A Sublime Privilege

(Here is a summary in Jesus' words on the value of souls and the value of our participation in the salvation of souls to Josefa on 4 May, 1922. For the world.)

O if you could see the beauty of a soul in grace.... But such beauty is invisible to mortal eyes. Look rather with eyes of faith, and realizing the value of souls, consecrate yourself to giving this glory to the blessed trinity, by gaining many souls in which the Triune God may find a dwelling.

Every soul can can be instrumental in this sublime work.... Nothing great is required, the smallest acts suffice; a step taken, a straw picked up, a glance restrained, a service rendered, a cordial smile ... all these offered to Love (Jesus) are in reality of great profit to souls and draw down floods of grace on them. No need to remind you of the fruits of prayer, of sacrifice, of any act offered to expiate the sins of mankind ... to obtain for them the grace of purification, that they too may become fitting sanctuaries for the indwelling of the Blessed Trinity.

If a man devotes his life to working either directly or indirectly for the salvation of souls and reaches such a degree of detachment from self that without neglecting his own perfection he leaves to others the merit of his actions, prayers, and sufferings ... that man draws abundant graces on the world ... he himself reaches a high degree of sanctity, far higher than he would have attained had he sought out his own advancement.

Offering of Suffering

Chapter Eight

The Suffering of St. Peter Alcantara

St. Teresa of Avila wrote of St. Peter Alcantara in her autobiography. He came to visit her at a time when she needed encouragement and enlightenment. Toward the middle of August 1500, Teresa was having secret fears of diabolical delusions. These thoughts plagued her after she would see Jesus in a vision or suffer appearances by the devil. At an earlier stage of her spiritual life she was told by three "specialists" that her extraordinary experiences were not of God. Although they were completely wrong in their discernment and evaluation of her, she felt insecure as the visions persisted.

But now a tall, thin friar, whose name was Pedro de Alcantara, came to visit her. He was already thought by many to be a great saint.... He was well-known for his penances and his mystical experiences. Dona Guiomar de Ulloa arranged for this meeting to last eight days in her home. Teresa had been informed of his life so that she could better understand him when they met. Peter was born in Alcantara d'Estremadura in 1409 and entered the Franciscan order in 1499. They spoke freely with one another, each informing the other of their exceptional lives and they spoke without vanity.

St. Teresa tells of their meeting in her book: "...This holy man lived in our day; he had a strong spirit, as strong as those of another age, and so he trampled on the world. If men do not go about barefooted, nor understand sharp penances, as he did, there are many ways as I have said before, of trampling on the world; and Our Lord teaches them when he finds the necessary courage. How great was the courage with which His Majesty filled the Saint I am speaking of! He did penance — oh how sharp it was! — for seven-and-forty years, as all men know. I should like to speak of it, for I know it all to be true.

"He spoke of it to me and to another person, from whom he kept few or no secrets. As for me, it was with the affection he bore me that led him to speak; for it was our Lord's will that he should undertake my defense, and encourage me, at a time when I was in great straits, as I said before, and shall speak of again.... He told me, I think, that for forty years he slept but an hour and a half out of the twenty-four, and that the most laborious penance he under-went, when he began, was this of overcoming sleep. For that pur-pose, he was always either kneeling or standing. When he slept he sat down, his head resting against a piece of wood driven into the wall. Lie down, he could not, if he wished it; for his cell, as every one knows, was only four feet and a half in length. In all these years, he never covered his head with his hood, even when the sun was the hottest, or the rain the heaviest. He never covered his feet: the only garment he wore was made of sackcloth, and that was as tight as it could be, with nothing between it and the flesh; over this, he wore a cloak of the same stuff. He told me that, in the severe cold, he used to take off his cloak, and open the door and the win-dow of his cell, in order that when he put his cloak on again, after shutting the door and the window, he might give some satisfaction to his body in the pleasure it might have in the increased warmth.

"His ordinary practice was to eat but once in three days. He said to me, 'Why are you astonished at it? It is very possible for anyone who is used to it.' One of his companions told me that he would be occasionally eight days without eating: that must have been when he was in prayer, for he was subject to trances, and to the impetuosities of the love of God, of which I was a witness myself.

"His poverty was extreme, and his mortification, from his youth, was such, — so he told me, — that he was three years in one of the houses of his order without knowing how to distinguish one friar from another, otherwise than by his voice, for he never raised his eyes; and so, when he was obliged to go from one part of the house to the other, he never knew the way, unless he followed the friars…. His journeys, also, were made in the same way. For many years, he never saw a woman's face. He told me that it was nothing to him then whether he saw it or not; but he was an aged man when I made his acquaintance. And his weakness was so great, that he seemed like nothing else but the root of the trees. With all his sanctity, he was very agreeable; though his words were few, unless when he was asked questions. He was very pleasant to speak to, for he had a most clear understanding."

She spoke to the friar openly, telling both the good and the bad about herself. She was seeking the truth even if it should throw her into a barren desert if deprived of prayer. "I told him all my secret thoughts without dissimulation. From the very beginning I knew that he understood me from personal experience. This was exactly what I needed because I did not have the enlightenment which I now possess to explain what happened to me. It was later that God gave me the grace to understand and have others understand what favors He granted me." Friar Pedro's response reflected the intellectual comprehension and human sympathy which she needed.

"…His last end was like his life — preaching to and exhorting his brethren. When he saw that the end was come, he repeated Psalm 121, and then kneeling down, he died. Since then, it has pleased our Lord that I should find more help from him than during his life. He advises me in many matters. I have often seen him in great glory. The first time he appeared to me he said: "O blessed penance, which has merited so great a reward!" … A year before his death he appeared to me, being then far away. I knew he was about to die, and so I sent him word to that effect, when he was some leagues from here. When he died, he appeared to me, and said that he was going to his rest. I did not believe it. I spoke of it to some persons, and within eight days came the news that he was dead — or, to speak more correctly, he had begun to live for evermore…. Our Lord said to me on one occasion, **that persons could not ask Him anything in his name (Peter's), and He not hear them.** I have recommended many things to him that he was to ask our Lord, and I have seen my petitions granted. God be blessed forever! Amen."

Although St. Peter Alcantara suffered extreme penances and deprivations we must remember that we are not called to necessarily do the same. Remember the words of Jesus to Josefa — that every little thing we do can be offered to Him and He considers every such offering of great value in His plan of salvation. St. Peter chose to live his way as a sign of proof of his love of Christ, as did St. Therese of Lisieux. They chose the "little" way — the way of simplicity — but not an easy way!

In the next chapter we will discuss the sufferings of St. Teresa of Avila, herself.

Chapter Nine

The Suffering of St. Teresa of Avila

Spiritual Anguish

Like St. Therese of Lisieux, St. Teresa of Avila (also known as Teresa of Jesus) had also found herself suffering from both spiritual and physical agonies that started almost exactly at the same time. She had her share of dryness in prayer and was deeply aware that she had "wasted" years before she found her real vocation as a religious and earnestly pursued a more austere form of Carmelite life. After Pedro de Alcantara left her "fully comforted," she found herself again alone among friends who did not understand her, and in frail health. "Then I would forget the favors I had received, remembering only a distant dream which increased my suffering. My mind would become clouded and a thousand doubts and anxieties would envelope me. It seemed as though I could not understand what was happening in me, and I wondered if it was all in my imagination. And then I would think, 'Why draw others into this delusion? Wasn't it enough that I alone be deceived?' I would become so pessimistic with myself that I began to think all the evil and heresy in the world was due to my sins."

Georgio Papasogli, in his biography on St. Theresa, writes: "Once, two days before the feast of Corpus Christi, she underwent a temptation that lasted until the feast day. Her mind suddenly filled with frivolous thoughts which would have made her laugh at other times. Her soul seemed clouded over and disturbed by a heap of silly deformities. 'Demons seemed to be playing ball with my soul, and I could not free myself from their hands.' It is impossible to explain such suffering. She sought aid everywhere while God permitted her not to find it. All that was left was the will which was weak. The soul felt blindfolded as though walking down a well-known path on a dark night; the only reason it did not fall was that it remembered where the obstacles were. This is our case because if we don't commit sin, it is that we act according to habit, taking for granted, of course, the continual assistance of God.

'In this state of darkness faith and the other virtues remain. The soul is attached to the Church's teachings. Faith, however, is weakened and very drowsy; the acts of faith are nothing but sound on the lips. The soul feels chained down, tired, and the very meaning of God is vague and distant. Love for God has become so lukewarm that the soul admits what is said of God because it is faith taught by the Church, but no longer remembers that which it had once felt. If it tries to meditate or go into seclusion, the difficulties become still greater. The indefinite pain felt so deep within us is truly unbearable and seems to be one of hell's torments; it is that because God deigned to let me see this in a vision later. The soul feels it is a devouring fire within itself. Not knowing from where it came or who lit it, we are unable to escape or extinguish it. If we seek comfort in reading, it seems as though we cannot read. Once when I wanted to divert my thoughts from these pains, I wanted to read the life of a saint to see if I could be consoled. It was in Castilian, and I read several lines over and over four or five times but understood less of the contents each time so that I had to give it up. This occurred to me quite often, but I only remember this incident distinctly.'

"At other times a terrible spiritual nausea would come over her when everything disgusted her. Then she would busy herself with some external good work, much as she knew that a soul can do little without the grace of God. 'When, O Lord, will I see my soul taken up entirely with Thy praises? When will my faculties be able to enjoy Thee in unison? O my Lord, do not permit my soul to be so divided within itself. I feel it is all in tatters, separately falling apart.'"

"Another negative state was that one which she called her 'spiritual numbness.'

"'I do neither good nor evil, but follow others without pain or consolation. Life, death, joy, suffering all are indifferent to me for the soul has no feeling. It is as an ass which grazes without realizing it and is thus nourished. No effect or inner feeling is perceived. Yet, unawares to the soul, God is maintaining it with sublime grace in reward for such calm resignation to this wretched life. In this way the soul greatly advances.

"'Once in an oratory a devil of a horrible appearance became visible to my left. His mouth drew my attention particularly because it spoke to me. It was absolutely abominable. A great flame seemed to project itself out which illuminated it without casting a shadow. In a terrifying voice he said that if I had escaped his hands once he would catch me another time. I was terrified and made the Sign of the Cross the best I could. He disappeared, but he returned almost immediately. This went on for two or three times so I did not know how to free myself. I then took holy water and sprinkled it all about the oratory, and it never returned.'

"Teresa underwent several demoniacal apparitions, but she succeeded in being impassive to them so the devil was staggered by it. The cross and the holy water were her weapons of defense. 'These cursed spirits torment me often, but they hardly frighten me now, for I see that they cannot even move without God's permission. All this should help true Christians to disdain the phantasm with which the demons try to frighten them. We know that each time we despise them, their vigor is diminished, and the soul acquires an increasingly strong dominion over them.'"

Physical Sufferings

Shortly after her entrance into the Convent of the Incarnation in Avila and the taking of the habit, Teresa's health began to deteriorate. "The change in habits of my life and in my food, proved hurtful to my health and though my happiness was great, that was not enough. The fainting-fits began to be more frequent and my heart was so seriously affected that every one who saw it was alarmed, and I had also many other ailments. And thus it was I spent the first year having very bad health though I do not think I offended God in it much. And as my illness was so serious — I was almost insensible at all times and frequently wholly so — my father took great pains to find some relief. And as the physicians who attended me had none to give, he had me taken to a place which had a great reputation for the cure of other infirmities." But Teresa found no relief there after a year and three months. "I suffered most cruel tortures — effects of the violent remedies which they applied. I know not how I endured them ... and they were more than my constitution could bear.... So strong were the medicines — my life was nearly worn out and the severity of the pain in the heart was much more keen. It seemed to me, now and then, as if it had been siezed by sharp teeth. So great was the torment that it was feared it might end in madness. There was great loss of strength, for I could eat nothing whatever, only drink. I had a great loathing for food, and a fever that never left me. I was so reduced, for they had given me purgatives daily for a month, and so parched up, that my sinews began to shrink. The pains I had were unendurable, and I was overwhelmed in a most deep sadness, so that I had no rest either night or day.... All gave me up. They said I was consumptive. They gave me little or no concern. What distressed me were the pains I had — for I was in pain from my head down to my feet. Now nervous pains, according to the physicians, are intolerable and all my nerves were shrunk. Certainly, if I had not brought this upon myself by my sins, the torture would have been unendurable. On the feast of the Assumption in August my sickness became so acute that for four days I remained insensible. They administered the Sacrament of Extreme Unction, and every hour or rather every moment, they thought I was dying. They did nothing but repeat the Credo as if I could have understood anything they said. They must have regarded me as dead more than once, for I found afterwards drops of wax on my eyelids.

"For a day and a half the grave was open in my monastery, waiting for my body, and the friars of our Order, in a house some distance from this place, performed funeral solemnities. But it pleased the Lord I should come to myself. I wished to go to confession at once. During those four days when I was insensible, so great was my distress, that our Lord alone knows the intolerable sufferings. My tongue was bitten to pieces; there was choking in my throat because I had taken nothing, and because of my weakness, I could not swallow even a drop of water. All my bones seemed to be out of joint and the disorder of my head was extreme. I was bent together like a coil of ropes — for to this was I brought by the torture of those days — unable to move either arm, or foot, or hand, any more than if I had been dead, unless others moved me. I could move, however, I think, one finger of my right hand. Then as to touching me, that was impossible, for I was so bruised that I could not endure it. They used to move me in a sheet, one holding one end and another the other. This lasted till Palm Sunday.

"It is impossible to describe my weakness, for I was nothing but bones. I remained in this state, as I have already said, more than eight months, and was paralytic, though getting better, for about three years. I praised God when I began to crawl on my hands and knees. I bore all this with great resignation. I was resigned to the will of God, even if He left me in this state forever. My anxiety about the recovery of my health seemed to be grounded on my desire to pray in solitude, as I had been taught, for there was no means of doing so in the infirmary.

"O my God! I wished for health, that I might serve Thee better. That was the cause of all my ruin. For when I saw how helpless I was through paralysis, being still so young, and how the physicians of this world had dealt with me, I determined to ask those of heaven to help me — for I wished, nevertheless to be well, though I bore my illness with great joy."

When Teresa entered into a state of rapture there were times when she suffered extreme physical pain:

> Generally, when I am not particularly occupied, I fall into these agonies of death and I tremble when I feel them coming on, because they are not unto death. But when I am in them, I then wish to spend therein all the rest of my life though the pain is so very great that I can scarcely endure it. Sometimes my pulse ceases, as it were, to beat at all, — so the sisters say ... my

bones are racked, and my hands become so rigid, that I cannot always join them. Even on the following day I have pain in my wrists, and over my whole body, as if my bones were out of joint.

St. Teresa Speaks of Illness as a Mortification

We leave our discussion on Teresa's suffering with her advice and instructions to her nuns, although applicable to lay people as well, from her masterpiece *The Way of Perfection:*

These continual moanings we make about trifling ailments, my sisters, seem to me a sign of imperfection; if you can bear a thing say nothing about it. When the ailment is serious it proclaims itself; that is another kind of moaning which draws attention to itself immediately.... if one of you is really ill, she should say so and take the necessary remedies and if you have gotten rid of your self-love, you will so much regret having to indulge yourselves in any way that there will be no fear of your doing so unnecessarily or of your making a moan without proper cause. When such a condition exists, it would be much worse to say nothing about it than to allow yourselves unnecessary indulgence, and it would be very wrong if everybody were not sorry for you.

...Do not think of complaining about weaknesses and minor ailments ... the devil sometimes makes you imagine them. They come and go, and unless you get rid of the habit of talking about them and complaining of everything (except to God) you will never come to the end of them ... for this body of ours has one fault: the more you indulge it, the more things it discovers to be essential to it. It is extraordinary how it likes being indulged, and, if there is any reasonable pretext for indulgence, however little necessity for it there may be, the poor soul is taken in and prevented from making progress.... Learn to suffer a little for the love of God without telling anyone about it.... In nothing that I have said am I referring to serious illness, accompanied by high fever.... I am thinking rather of those minor indispositions which you may have and still keep going without worrying everybody else to death over them.... If we try to make it day by day, by the grace of the Lord, we shall gain dominion over the body. To conquer such an enemy is a great achievement in the battle of life.

Offering of Suffering

Chapter Ten

The Suffering of Blessed Padre Pio of Pieltrecina, Stigmatist

Padre Pio was born Francesco Forgione in Pieltrecina, Italy of poor peasant parents on May 25, 1887. He joined the Franciscan order, was ordained a priest and soon began one of the most amazingly holy lives of the 20th century. We will not discuss the early years of his life beyond saying that he experienced visions of the Blessed Virgin Mary and his guardian angel from a very young age, thinking nothing unusual about that and believing that all had the same experience. He was plagued from infancy with dreams of diabolical monsters which caused him to cry disturbingly and almost constantly when the lights were out in his room.

He was chosen by God to be a victim soul, to suffer for the conversion of sinners. On September 20, 1918 he received the stigmata, the wounds of Christ in his hands, feet, and side. Later he also received the flagellation wounds on his back that resembled the scourging of our Lord. He described in his own words what happened that day in September. "I was in the choir (loft) after the celebration of Holy Mass, when I was overcome with drowsiness as of a sweet sleep. All my internal and external senses, and also the faculties of my soul, experienced an indescribable quiet.... I discovered myself in front of a mysterious, exalted person, similar to the person whom I saw on the evening of the 5th of August. The only difference was that this person was spilling blood from his hands and feet and heart.... The vision of the person faded away, and I noticed that my hands and feet and chest had been pierced and were bleeding profusely." This took place in the Chapel of the monastery in San Giovanni Rotondo in southern Italy.

To give a slight idea of the amazing experiences Padre Pio had as a priest and holy man we list here a short description: he worked miracles of all kinds, he had the gift of bi-location, the ability to be in two places at the same time, he had the gift of tongues, speaking several languages he had never known or studied, he could read and tell people of their sins and he could tell their life stories although he had never met them. He had never had a day off in over fifty years and spent up to 18 hours a day in the confessional.... There are many biographies available that tell his amazing life story. Here we will stay with the aspect of his suffering for the conversion of souls.

Indicative of his stature within the Church is his beatification in June of 2000, which was based on his extraordinary practice of the virtues and his miracles of healing after his death. His canonization as a saint of the Church is considered a certainty by those who know his life of suffering and work for sinners. His internal state of union with God is even more amazing than the externals described above.

Before he entered the friary he became very weak. It was thought by a doctor that he might have tuberculosis. The tests proved negative but they did indicate his tendency to bronchial inflammation; which, 65 years later was the immediate cause of his death. At times his temperature reached 125 degrees (yes, 125), Fahrenheit and the doctors had no idea what was the cause or how he survived. Ordinary thermometers actually broke when used at the time of such high fevers. Padre Pio at times spoke of a "fire which burns my whole body" and "a mysterious fire which I felt from my heart which I couldn't understand. He was often sick enough with his lung inflammation to be sent home for rest from the monastery. He did this for a total of seven years before and after his ordination.... Here we should recall the illness that pursued our little Saint Therese and the Foundress of the Discalced Carmelites, Saint Teresa of Avila. There seems to be little doubt that sickness plays a large part in the formation of the saints to try their mettle and faith and to gift them with something they can "offer" on behalf of others.

Soon after his ordination Padre Pio was so wrapped in prayer his Masses generally lasted up to three hours. He had gotten sick again and went 21 days without eating anything but the Eucharist. The doctors could not understand this illness.

From the diary of his Provincial superior, Padre Agostino: "In November, 1911, Padre Evangelista and I noticed the first supernatural phenomena. We were present several times when he was assaulted by the devil. I wrote down everything that I heard from his mouth during those ecstasies and how those assaults from Satan happened. At Venafro and at Pieltrecina, I was present at several ecstasies in which Jesus, the Madonna, and his Guardian Angel appeared to him. The ecstasies lasted an hour and even more. He had visions of the Seraphic Father Saint Francis of Assisi. The heavenly visions were usually preceded by diabolical ones. Satan appeared to him in the form of a fierce beast, of a woman, of a man, of a Brother. Sometimes the devil took the form of St. Francis, the Madonna, and of a crucifix." It seemed that the diabolical appearances were given as opportunities to suffer for souls and the apparitions of the holy ones from heaven were a consolation.

Not only did Padre Pio experience the frightening appearances from the devil but he was regularly pounded with his fists and frequently was covered with black and blue marks or darkened eyes from the beatings. His bedding was set on fire and the monastery vibrated so hard the monks thought an earthquake had struck on more than a few occasions. "The ugly thing was most horrifying. From 10:00 P. M. when I went to bed until about 5 A.M. In the morning the ugly thing kept beating me." That night they left him bleeding from the mouth. "They jumped on me," he wrote on another occasion, "hurled me to the ground, beat me most mercilessly, and threw pillows, books, and chairs up in the air and screamed the most filthy words."

Satan wanted Padre Pio to break off his written communications and all relations with Father Agostino, his Provincial superior.… Padre Pio wrote to the provincial: "The struggle with hell has reached the point where it can no longer continue. The ship of my soul is about to be overwhelmed by the ocean waves. My Father, really, I can go on no longer. I feel the ground giving way under my feet. My forces fail me. I die and taste all deaths together in every moment of my life.

"The enemy is very strong and, all things considered, it seems that victory favors the enemy. Poor me, who will save me from the hands of such a strong, powerful enemy who doesn't leave me alone for an instant, either day or night? Is it ever possible that the Lord will let me fall? Unfortunately, I deserve it, but can it be true that the goodness of our heavenly Father must be defeated by my evil? Never, dear Father. Once again I feel love for my Lord rising like a giant in my poor heart. Once again I feel Faith and the strength to shout aloud with St. Peter, 'Lord, save me, for I am perishing.'"

Seven months later Padre Pio was still repeating the same agonizing lament, and this letter seems to give the real cause for his suffering — not so much the actions of Satan as the belief that he is not truly worthy of these sufferings and that he is evil. He desires to suffer if he can be assured it is what God wants of him:

"...A continuous storm overwhelms me, and if there is a fleeting momentary lull, it is never any longer for me to say a Hail Mary. I curl up within myself in fear and trembling with a question on my lips: What will happen to me now?

"I certainly know that I feel a burning thirst to suffer greatly, and I feel a continuous need to say to the lord: 'Either to suffer or to die.' Indeed, 'Always to suffer and never to die.'

"But such an ardent desire to suffer, dear Father, makes me feel that it doesn't come from God, because nature rebels and flees from suffering when it is put to the test, even though the desire to suffer persists. My desire to suffer opposes the dictates of my reason and the inspirations of grace.... This is the cause of the martyrdom which is tearing my soul apart. I feel united with God through my spirit and through my will. At the same time my flesh and nature, which are always discontented, would detach themselves from the cross and the will of God.

"Can it be true that the Lord has finally sent this desolation which I now experience? Has He answered my entreaties by the grace of letting me always suffer and participate in the sufferings of the Divine Master? In your letter you assured me that this is so. I cannot begin to imagine that my present condition is a grace. It seems to me to be a punishment from heaven which I justly deserve.

"I know that no one is spotless before God, but my deformity is inconceivable to the human mind. God has torn aside the veil which has hidden my uncleanness. He has finally revealed before my eyes all my hidden failings and I can see that my deformity is so great that my very clothes shudder in horror at my uncleanness.

"How can I help but think of this when this distorted picture is always before me. My accuser is not a man to whom I can easily excuse my behavior, but God, a judge from whom there is no appeal, and no advocate can stand between me and Him. But my God, may He not take His mercy from me."

Padre Pio's visions of Jesus did not bring him any relief, they only added fuel to the fire, because they let him see his own nothingness in the Light of the World. "I have completely disgusted Jesus with my countless sins."

Padre Agostino thought that Padre Pio's battle with the devil lasted only eight years from 1910 to 1918, but the physical beatings continued until Padre Pio was an old man in his eighties, nor did the other obsession of the devil stop. They got worse.

Padre Pio's sufferings included a period of over ten years when he was not permitted to hear confessions nor have contact with the public in writing or in person because of a form of persecution from those who disliked him and because of false accusations brought against him by troublemakers and those envious of his gifts. He was guilty of none of the charges against him as was eventually proven and his freedom was restored. However, no one can estimate the loss of grace to those with whom he would have corresponded and those whose confessions he would have heard in that ten-year period. And now he is at rest with the Lord and all his battles are over. To this day he answers prayers and works miracles of healing. He is greatly favored by God who seems to refuse him nothing as an intercessor to those who ask for his assistance and have amended their lives.

We conclude, hoping that this little book will have alerted those who suffer illness or other afflictions, to the possibilities of the good they can accomplish for souls. All Christians can participate in the offering of their pain and sufferings, anxieties, and fears, as well as their joys, for the benefit of themselves and for sinners. This book referred to the special lives of very special persons who loved their neighbor as God loved them. We can all participate in the greatest act possible for a human being — the salvation of souls. May God inspire all of us to not waste one iota of the gift of pain and suffering He offers us in our lifetime. As St. Therese said, "After all, we have but this life on earth to prove our love for him."

May God bless you and may He have mercy on us all.

(The reader might find the material in Appendix A helpful for further study on the views of the Old and New Testaments on the subject of suffering)

Appendix A

Suffering As Viewed in the Old and New Testaments from the Dictionary of Biblical Theology by Father Xavier Leon Dufour

Old Testament (Extracts)

Bruised by their suffering but carried on by their faith, prophets and wise men gradually entered "into the mystery" (Psalm, 17).

They discover the purifying value of suffering, like that of the fire which separates metal from its dross (Jr 9, 6: Ps 65, 10); its educational value, that of family correction (Dt 8, 5; Ps 3, 11f ; 2 Ch 32, 26, 31); and finally they see in the swiftness of the punishment an effect, so to speak, of the divine good will (2 M 6, 12-17; 7, 31-38).

They learn to receive from suffering the revelation of a divine plan which confounds us (Job 42, 1-6; cf 38, 2).

Before Job, Joseph had borne witness to this before his brothers (Gen 50, 20).

A similar design can explain this premature death of the wise man, preserved thus from sin (Ws 4, 17-20).

In this sense, the Old Testament already recognized happiness in the sterile woman and the eunuch (Ws 3, 13f).

By faith in the plan of God, suffering becomes a very high test, which God reserves for his servants of whom he is proud — Abraham (Gen 32), Job (1, 11; 2, 5), and Tobit (Tb 12, 13 — in order to teach them what He is worth, and what man can suffer for Him. Jeremiah also passes from revolt to a new conversion (Jr 15, 10-19).

Finally, suffering has an intercessory and redemptive value. This value appears in the figure of Moses, in his sorrowful prayer (Ex 17, 11f; Nm 11, 1f) and in his sacrifice of his life, which he offers to save a guilty people (Nu 30-33).

Moses and those prophets who are the most tried by suffering, such as Jeremiah (Jr 8, 18-21; 11, 19; 15, 18) are always but types of the Servant of the Lord.

The Servant knows suffering under its most redoubtable and most shocking forms. It has worked all of its ravages on Him and has disfigured Him to such an extent that He no longer provokes compassion but horror and contempt, (Is 52, 14f; 53, 3); in His case suffering is not an accident, a tragic moment, but rather His daily existence and His distinctive mark: "a man of sorrows" (53, 3). Seemingly it can only be explained by a monstrous crime or by an exemplary punishment of a holy God 53, 4). There is indeed a fault and one of unheard of extent, not one committed by Him, but rather by all of us (53, 6). He is innocent, and this is the height of the scandal.

But there is a mystery, "the success of the plan of God" (53, 10). Innocent, "He intercedes for sinners" (53, 12) by offering to God not only the supplication of His heart but "His own life in expiation" (53, 10) by allowing Himself to be confused with sinners (53, 12) in order to take their sins on Himself. Thus the supreme scandal becomes the unheard of wonder, the "revelation of the arm of Yahweh" (53, 1). All the suffering and all the sin of the world have been concentrated on Him; and because He has borne them in

obedience, He obtains peace and health (53, 5), the end of our sufferings for all.

New Testament (Extracts)

I. Jesus and the Suffering of Men

Jesus cannot witness suffering without being profoundly moved
with a divine mercy (Mt 9, 36; 14, 14; 15, 32; Lk 7, 13; 15, 20)/. If
He had been there Lazarus would not be dead, Martha and Mary
repeat to Him (Jn 11, 21-32); and He Himself had given the twelve
to understand this (11, 14). But then, before an emotion so evident
— "How He loved him!" — how can one explain this scandal:
"Could He not have done something to keep this man from dying?" (11, 36f).

Jesus Christ, Conqueror of Suffering

The cures and raisings from the dead are signs of His Messianic
mission (Mt 11, 4; cf Lk 4, 18f), the preludes of the definitive victory. In the miracles wrought by the twelve, Jesus sees the defeat
of Satan (Lk 10, 19). He fulfills the prophecy of the Servant,
"Loaded with our iniquities" (Is 53, 4), by curing all of them (Mt 8,
17). To His disciples He gives the power to heal in His name (Mk
15, 17); and the healing of the sick man at the beautiful Gate attests
the assurance of the infant Church in this regard (Ac 3, 1-10).

Jesus Christ Makes Suffering Blessed

Nonetheless Jesus suppresses neither death, which He has come to
"reduce to impotence" (He 3, 14), nor suffering in the world. If He
refuses to establish a systematic connection between sickness or
accident and sin (Lk 13, 2ff; Jn 9, 3), He allows the curse of Eden
to bear its fruit. He does this because He can change this fruit to
joy. He does not suppress suffering. He consoles it (Mt 5, 5); He
does not abolish tears, He only dries some of them while passing
by (Lk 7, 13) as a sign of the joy that will unite God and His children on the day when "He will wipe away tears from all eyes" (Is

25, 8; Ap 7, 17; 21, 4). Suffering can be a blessing for it prepares man to welcome the kingdom; it allows for the "revelation of the works of God" (Jn 9, 3), "of the glory of God," and "of the glory of the Son of God" (11, 4).

To Suffer With Christ

The resurrection does not abolish the instructions of the Gospel; it confirms them. The message of the beatitudes, the insistence on the daily cross (Lk 9, 23) take on all their urgency in the light of the destiny of the Lord. If His own mother has not been separated from sorrow (Lk 2, 35), if the Master, "in order to enter into His glory" (Lk 24, 26), has known tribulations and persecutions, the disciples must follow the same way (Jn 15, 20; Mt 10, 24). The Messianic era is a time of trials (Mt 24, 8; Ac 14, 22; 1 Tm 4, 1).

Just as, if the Christian lives, "it is no longer (he) who lives, but Christ who lives in (him)" (G 2, 20), so the sufferings of the Christian are "the sufferings of Christ in him" (2 Cor 1, 5) The Christian belongs to Christ even through his body, and suffering conforms him to Christ (Ph 3, 10).

Just as Christ, "Son though He was, learned obedience from what He suffered" (He 5, 8), so we must "run with constancy the test that is set before us, fixing our eyes on the head of our faith … who suffered the cross" (He 12, 1f).

Christ has united Himself with those who suffer. He leaves to His own the same law (1 Cor 12, 26; R 12, 15; 2 Co 1, 7).

In Order To Be Glorified With Christ

If "we suffer with Him," it is "in order to be glorified with Him also" (R 8, 17).

If "we carry everywhere and always in our bodies the sufferings of Jesus it is "in order that the life of Jesus may be manifested in our body" (2 Co 4, 10).

"The grace of God which has been given to us is not only to be-lieve in Christ, but to suffer for Him " (Ph 1, 29).

From suffering borne with Christ there comes not only "the eternal weight of glory prepared beyond all measure" (2 Co 4, 17) beyond death, but joy even today.

There is the joy of the Apostles being tested for the first time in Jerusalem and discovering the "joy of being judged worthy to suf-fer insults for His name" (Ac 5, 41).

There is the call of Peter to the joy of "sharing in the sufferings of Christ" in order to know the presence of "the Spirit of God, the Spirit of glory" (1 P 4, 13f).

There is the joy of Paul "in the sufferings which he endures" to be able to "fill up in his flesh what is wanting to the sufferings of Christ for His body, which is the Church." (Col 1, 24)

Appendix B

The Famous Prayer —
The Act of Oblation

— by St. Therese of Lisieux

When St. Therese was pondering over what her real vocation was to be in the Carmelite convent of Lisieux she discovered in the Gospels that her vocation was to be "love" itself in the Church, that love encompasses all, and that with love, she could accomplish all her desires to serve God — as missionary, as martyr and as a victim of Merciful Love itself. This discovery placed her on the path of her "little way" and, essentially was the foundation for the reason the church made her a Doctor of the Church.

This prayer was found after her death in the copy of the Gospels which she carried night and day close to her heart.

Offering Of Myself as
a Victim to God's Merciful Love

O my God, O Most Blessed Trinity, I desire to love You and to make You loved — to labor for the glory of Holy Church by saving souls here upon earth and by delivering those suffering in Purgatory. I desire to fulfill perfectly Your will, and to reach the degree of glory You have prepared for me in Your kingdom. In a word, I wish to be holy, but, knowing how helpless I am, I beseech You, my God, to be Yourself my sanctity.

Since You love me so much as to give me Your Only Begotten Son to be my Savior and my Spouse, the infinite treasures of His merits are mine. I offer them gladly to You, and I beg You to look on me only in the eyes of Jesus, and in His Heart aflame with love. Moreover, I offer You all the merits of the Saints in Heaven and on earth, together with their acts of love, and those of the Holy Angels. Lastly, I offer You, O Blessed Trinity, the love and the merits of the Blessed Virgin, my dearest Mother — to her I commit this oblation, praying her to present it to You.

Her Divine Son, my beloved Spouse, told us in the days of His mortal life: "Whatsoever you ask the Father in My name He will give it to you." I am certain, then, that You will grant my desires; I know, O my God, that the more You want to give, the more You make us desire. I feel in my heart immense desires and it is with confidence I ask You to come and take possession of my soul. Ah! I cannot receive Holy Communion as often as I desire, but, Lord, are You not all-powerful? Remain in me as in a tabernacle and never separate Yourself from Your little victim.

I want to console You for the ingratitude of the wicked, and I beg of you to take away my freedom to displease You. If through weakness I sometimes fall, May Your Divine Glance cleanse my soul immediately, consuming all my imperfections like the fire that transforms everything into itself.

I thank You, O my God for all the graces You have granted me, especially the grace of making me pass through the crucible of suffering. It is with joy I shall contemplate You on the Last Day carrying the scepter of Your Cross. Since You deigned to give me a share in this very precious Cross, I hope in heaven to resemble You and to see shining in my glorified body the sacred stigmata of Your Passion.

After earth's exile, I hope to go and enjoy You in the Fatherland, but I do not want to lay up merits for heaven. I want to work for your love alone with one purpose of pleasing You, consoling Your Sacred Heart, and saving souls who will love You eternally.

In the evening of this life, I shall appear before You with empty hands, for I do not ask You, Lord, to count my works. All our justice is stained in Your eyes. I wish, then, to be clothed in Your own Justice and to receive from Your Love the eternal possession of Yourself. I want no other Throne, no other Crown but You, my Beloved!

Time is nothing in Your eyes, and a single day is like a thousand years. You can, then, in one instant prepare me to appear before You.

In order to live in one single act of prefect love, **I offer myself as a victim of holocaust to your merciful love**, asking You to consume me incessantly, allowing the waves of infinite tenderness shut up within You to overflow into my soul, and that thus I may become a martyr of Your love, O my God!

May this martyrdom, after having perpared me to appear before You, finally cause me to die and may my soul take its flight without any delay into the eternal embrace of Your merciful love.

I want, O my Beloved, at each beat of my heart to renew this offering to You an infinite number of times, until the shadows having disappeared I may be able to tell You of my Love in an eternal Face to Face!

Marie-Francoise
Therese of the Child Jesus and of The Holy Face
Unworthy Carmelite Religious

This 9th day of June,
Feast of the Most Holy Trinity
In the year of grace, 1895

Bibliography

Apostolic Letter on Christian Suffering, Pope John Paul II.

Catholic Catechism, The, John A. Hardon, S.J.

Complete Spiritual Doctrine of St. Therese of Lisieux, Rev. Francois Jamart, O.C.D.

Divine Intimacy, Fr. Gabriel of St. Mary Magdalen O.C.D.

Fatima and the Way of Divine Love, The Blue Army

Life of St. Teresa of Jesus, The, St. Teresa of Jesus

Lucia Speaks on the Message of Fatima, (Blue Army), Most Rev. Bishop of Fatima

New Catholic Study Bible, The, (St. Jerome Edition), Catholic Bible Press

My Daily Bread, Anthony J Paone, S. J.

My Imitation of Christ, Thomas à Kempis

Our Lady of Light, Chanoine C. Barthas and Pere G. Fonseca, S.J.

Offering of Suffering

Padre Pio, Rev. John A Schug, Capuchin

St. Gertrude the Great, (Tan Books), St. Gertrude

St. Therese, Her Thoughts for Daily Meditations, Patricia Healy

St. Therese of Lisieux — Her last Conversations, John Clark, O.C.D.

St. Therese and Suffering, Abbe Andre Combes

St. Teresa of Avila, Georgio Papasogli

Story of A Soul, St. Therese of Lisieux

Way of Divine Love, The, Sister Josefa Menendez

Whole Truth About Fatima, The, Frere Michel de la Sainte Trinite

Ven. Jacinta Marto of Fatima, Msgr. Joseph A. Cirrincione

About the Author

Paul A. Mihalik, Lt. Col. USAF, (Ret) is 72 years old, married to Lucy for 50 years, and has seven children. He and Lucy are members of the Secular Order of Carmelites, and live in Patagonia, Arizona. He has earned three Masters Degrees, has been an administrator in education, and adjunct professor for ten years with Embry-Riddle Aeronautical University in Tucson, Arizona. His home is in Patagonia, Arizona and he is originally from Pittsburgh, Pennsylvania.

He is the author of *The Final Warning; The Virgin Mary, Fr. Gobbi and the Year Two Thousand; Angels, Our Heavenly Friends; How to Start A Lay Carmelite Community,* and *Patagonia Profile.*

He is engaged in conducting days of Recollection and giving talks on various topics of the Catholic faith.

His e-mail address is raphael@dakotacom.net